for my wife,
Margarita
and daughters,
Martha and Victoria,
who brighten my life

Slovenian Axis Forces in World War II 1941-1945

by Antonio J. Munoz
(plate illustrations by Vincent Wai)

P. Stahl

Axis Europa Books

53-20 207th Street,
Bayside, N.Y. 11364
USA

ISBN- 1-891227-04-1

phone/fax: 1 (718) 229-1352

Internet: http://members.aol.com/axiseurope/index.htm

Printed in Canada

Acknowledgments

I would like to express my thanks to the following individuals and institutions, without which this book could never have been written. Let me thank Professors Dejan Voncina, Vanya Martincic, and Matija Zgajnar, all of the Museum of Modern History, Ljubljana, Slovenia. Their translations of documents and photographic asistance proved vital in completing this study. Also of assistance was the US National Archives, who supplied rolls of microfilm from which numerous documents are cited in this study. Individuals whom I am also indebted to include Mr. Nigel Thomas, Rudolf Pencz, Vincent Wai, Michael Wiener, and Dr. Hans Werner Neulen.

Very little has been written about the Slovenian Axis forces in World War II. This is especially true of any English language titles. To my knowledge, there are only two English language books which partially covers this theme: Nigel Thomas & Krunoslav Mikulan's "Axis Forces in Yugoslavia, 1941-45", and Marian Furlan's "Republika Slovenia." The following is a listing of the primary sources used for this study:

----"Zbornik Fotografij Iz Narodnoosvobodilnega Boja Slovenskega Narodna 1941-1945" Institut Za Zgodovino Delavskega Gibanja Muzej Narodne Osvoboditve LRS V Ljubljani: Arhitekt Vlasto Kopac, 1961. Three volumes.

Ferenc, Tone. "Razstava Ob Petdesetletnici Konca Druge Svetovne Vojne". Muzej Novejse Zgodovine: Ljubljana, 1995.

Franz, Hermann. "Gebirgsjaeger der Polizei. Polizei-Gebirgs-jaeger-Regiment 18 und Polizei-Gebirgsjaeger-Artillerie-abteilung 1942 bis 1945." Verlag Hans-Henning Podzun: Bad Nauheim. 1963.

Furlan, Marian. "Rupublika Slovenia Army Insignia & Decorations 1918-1992." Militaria House: Toronto, 1993.

Hartungen, Christoph von. "Die Suedtiroler Polizeiregimenter 1943-1945", n.d.

Kaltenegger, Roland. "Operationszone 'Adriatisches Kuestenland'. Der Kampf um Triest, Istrien und Fiume 1944-45." Leopold Stocker Verlag: Graz, 1993.

Kelpec, Matjaz. "Tuechern ist getraenkt mit unserem Blut. Das Schicksal der Heimwehrmaenner (Domobranci)." Selbstverlag, Editorial Baraga, SRL: Buenos Aires, 1973.

Littlejohn, David. "Foreign Legions of the Third Reich, Volume 3 - Albania, Czechoslovakia, Greece, Hungary and Yugoslavia." R. James Bender Publishing: San Jose, 1985.

Martincic, Vanya. "Slovenski Partizan. Orozje, obleka in oprema slovenskih partizanov." Muzej Ijudske revolucije Slovenije: Ljubljana, 1990.

Munoz, Antonio J. Twilight War: Northern Italy, 1945." in "Command Magazine,":San Luis Obispo, July-August, 1994, Issue 29, Pages 72-85.

--------, "The German Police." Axis Europa Books: Bayside, 1997.

Stuhlpfarrer, Karl von. "Die Operationszone 'Alpenvorland' und 'Adriatisches Kuestenland' 1943-1945." Verlag Brueder Holliner: Wien, 1969.

Thomas, Nigel & Krunoslav Mikulan. "Axis Forces in Yugoslavia, 1941-45." Osprey Men At Arms: London, 1995.

Vriser, Sergej. "Uniforme V Zgodovini. Slovenija In Sosednje Dezele." Partizanska knjiga: Ljubljana, 1987.

Publisher's Note

It is with great pleasure that I present "Slovenian Axis Forces in World War II, 1941-1945." This work presents the culmination of four years of publishing experience and research through our young editorial house, Axis Europa Books; All brought together in this one volume. I hope that you, the reader, will enjoy the fruits of our efforts.

Antonio J. Munoz,
author & publisher
Axis Europa Books
Axis Europa Magazine

ABOVE: A Slovenian wartime propaganda cartoon, taken from the war. It depicts a Slovenian White Guard volunteer, stabbing his fellow Slovene farmer in the back, while a German & Italian soldier are attacking him.

BELOW: The words read "In the name of Christ," and is meant to imply the Catholic Church's "complicity" with the Slovenian collaborationist forces. Definitely another Slovenian (Communist) partisan propaganda drawing from the war.

V KRISTUSOVEM IMENU !

Table of Contents

Introduction

In November 1918 the Habsburg Empire was on the brink of collapse. This supranational empire, where different nations, races and religions had lived together in harmony, had fought for its survival fiercely and courageously for four years to the utter surprise of its enemies in London, Paris, and St. Petersburg.

When everything seemed lost a Croatian officer, Field Marshal Svetozar Boroevic de Bojna, wanted to help his Austrian Emperor-King, Karl in his desperate situation and to regain Karl's freedom of action by occupying Vienna with the well disciplined Army of the Isonzo. But this last act of fidelity and heroism never occurred.

Boroevic's plan was the last attempt of resistance of a supranational idea against secessionism and nationalism, which began to rule the fate of the countries emerging from the ruins of the Danube monarchy. The "pax austriaca" which, when recalled nostalgically, looked like a paradise of multinational diversity in European unity, was not replaced by a balanced and just postwar order, but by the Treaty of Versailles and its version of peace.

The Kingdom of Yugoslavia - until 1929 it was named the Kingdom of the Serbs, Croats and Slovenes - was the heir of the ruined Austro-Hungarian double monarchy in the Balkans. It gained the territories of southern Styria, Kraina, Croatia, Slavonia, Bosnia-Herzegovina, and the bulk of Dalmatia. This "product of Versailles" was an ethnic hodgepodge which contained Serbians (45% of the population), Croatians, Slovenians, Germans, Hungarians, Romanians, Bulgarians, Greeks, Albanians, and Turks.

Nearly until the end of the state, the kingdom's leadership never considered giving the minorities a chance to participate meaningfully in the government. Serbian centralism dominated over Croatian and Slovenian wishes for autonomy and federalism. Their unfulfilled hopes created an explosive mixture. in 1929, internal tensions in Yugoslavia caused the dismissal of the parliament and the establishment of a dictatorship by the Serbian King.

Five years later the first nationalist reaction to this dictatorship exploded. Croatian extremists murdered the Serbian King, Alexander Ist in Marseilles, France.[1] Only in August, 1939 did Belgrade concede to address the "Croat question," and gave the Croatians some independence, although this move was too little and too late to really achieve a reconciliation between the Serbs and Croats, or to assure the kingdom of Yugoslavia's survival in the field of international policy.

Mussolini's attack on Greece on October 29th, 1940 changed the map and balance of power in the Balkans. Hitler decided to act, when the Greek counterattacks drove the Italians back and entered Italian controlled Albania. Hitler needed stability in the southeastern flank for his upcoming invasion of the Soviet Union. In 1940, National Socialist Germany had no territorial claims in Yugoslavia, but wanted to trade with her for its economic resources, and was therefore interested in a stable southern Slavic state.

Germany therefore planned to integrate Yugoslavia into its Axis system. The Belgrade government and Prince Paul hesitated, basically because they feared internal unrest if Yugoslavia would side with Berlin and Rome. Finally, German pressure and the promise to support Yugoslav claims for the Greek port of Saloniki turned the scale. On March 25th, 1941 the Yugoslavian prime minister,

---

[1] The actual assassination was carried out by Macedonian extremists from IMRO (The Inner Macedonian Revolutionary Organization), which was acting on behalf of the Croatians. IMRO also sought autonomy and freedom for Macedonia from the Serbian-dominated Yugoslav government. For more details, see "Herakles & the Swastika: Greek Volunteers in the German Army, Police & SS, 1943-45" by Antonio J. Munoz. Axis Europa: Bayside, 1996. ISBN: 1-891227-06-8.

Cvetkovic signed the treaty initiating Yugoslavia into the Axis fold.

The ink on this treaty had just dried, when two days after its signing, a pro-western coup toppled the Cvetkovic Administration and King Peter II ascended to the Serbian throne. The coup was clearly anti-German, a fact which was confirmed by isolated excesses against German individuals and institutions. The National Socialist leadership in Berlin reacted swiftly, uncompromisingly, and brutally: Already on March 27th Hitler had given orders to smash the Yugoslav state and to destroy Belgrade using the *Luftwaffe* (German Air Force).

German units massed in Hungary, Romania, and Bulgaria. The attacking forces - composed of the 12th and 2nd German armies - had air support of about 900 planes. The offensive against Yugoslavia and Greece began on April 6th, 1941. Italian troops, and from April 11th on also, Hungarian troops assisted the German forces. The Yugoslav Army with its forces made up of different nationalities broke down, not only from enemy pressure, but also because of internal frictions.

The Croatian ultra-nationalists Pavelic and Kvaternik (who was a former Colonel in the Croatian Army) proclaimed an independent state in Zagreb beginning on April 10th. The Kingdom of Yugoslavia surrendered on April 17th. The victors now divided the country. Germany gained northern Slovenia and occupied old Serbia and the Banat, while Italy annexed southern Slovenia and parts of Dalmatia. It occupied Montenegro and western Macedonia and enlarged Albania, which was an Italian occupied territory since 1939.

Hungary gained the Backa (Bachka) and Baranya triangle, while Bulgarian troops entered eastern Macedonia. This swift victory led the victors to arrogance and over-confidence, especially when dealing with the Serbians. Hitler thought that in the German held territories a three-division occupation force would be sufficient.

New states and para-states emerged from the bankrupt estate of Yugoslavia. Being under Italian protection, the Independent State of Croatia, welcomed in the beginning by most of its inhabitants, had 6,300,000 people (1943), only 3,300,000 of them Catholic Croats. Whereas two million were Serbs and the rest "other" nationalities. The German occupation government in Serbia (which had 4,450,000 inhabitants in 1941) tolerated an indigenous government with a very limited authority, headed by General Milan Nedic beginning in August, 1941.

Small Montenegro, which had been independent from 1878 to 1918, had only 435,000 inhabitants and no government at all. Originally the Italians had planned to place the son of the last King of Montenegro on the throne, but installed an Italian "High Commissioner" in the town of Cetinje instead, when the King's son refused their offer. The stage for the future drama was now set.

Occupation troops of the four Axis forces, German National Socialists and Italian Fascists, Croatian nationalists and Croatian Communists, Serbian monarchists and Serbian Stalinists, Montenegrin separatists and Bosnian autonomists, exiled Russian followers of the Czar and Allied secret agents, Slovenian patriots and Macedonian revolutionaries, Catholics, Orthodox pan-Slavs, Muslims and Jews all acted on this tragic stage, set in the former territory that was known as the Kingdom of Yugoslavia.

Ethnic, social, religious and national conflicts overlapped and combined in a triangle that was really impossible to unravel. An elaborate policy of peaceful resettlement would have been necessary to smooth out all of these diverging tendencies and interests, or to subordinate them to a common, universal idea. But National Socialist Germany, the leading power of the Axis, was totally unfit for the role of mediator. The daring exploits of the German tank divisions through Europe had not been followed by an inspiring theory or doctrine.

The idea of anti-Semitism and anti-Communism, combined with propaganda of the superiority of Germans might have attracted a minority in Europe, but were

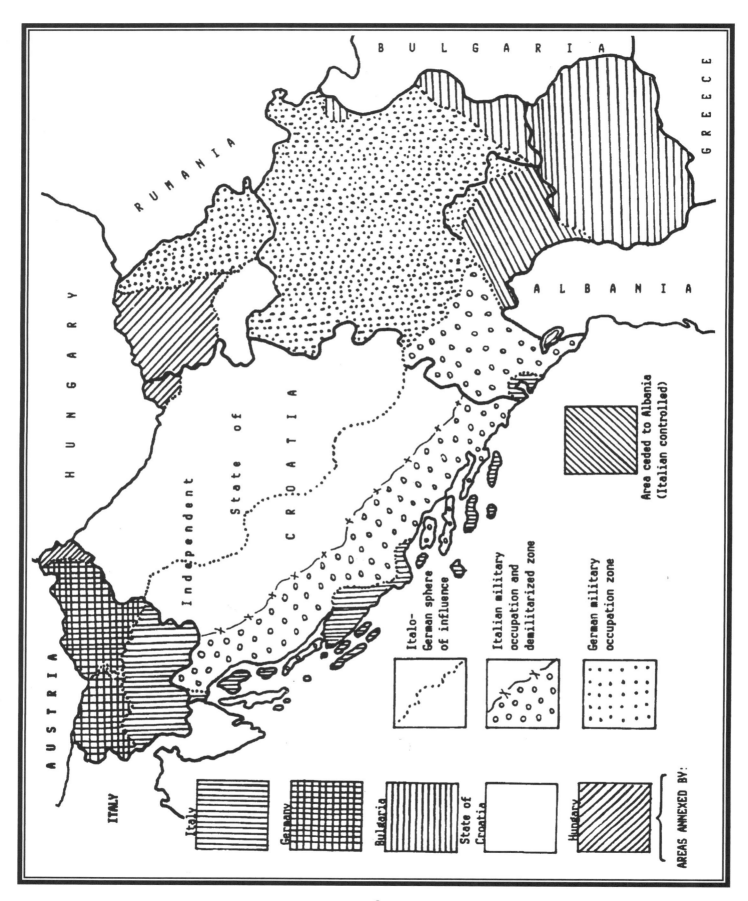

BULGARIA

GREECE

RUMANIA

ALBANIA

HUNGARY

Independent State of CROATIA

AUSTRIA

ITALY

Area ceded to Albania (Italian controlled)

Italo-German sphere of influence

Italian military occupation and demilitarized zone

German military occupation zone

Italy

Germany

Bulgaria

State of Croatia

Hungary

AREAS ANNEXED BY:

extremely useless for an ideology of integration into a European federation of states because they denied the equality of nations and designed a racist hierarchy as the New Order of Europe. There was no place for Jews and Slavs in this vague "New Order." Not all Slavs were destined for extermination, but they could not expect a special place in "new" Europe.

The former lawyer Dr. Ante Pavelic, leader of the radical Ustashe movement, which had been founded in 1929, wanted to extinguish the stain of south-Slavic origin of his people and encouraged scientists and publicists to "prove" the non-Slavic origin of the Croatian people. But no one in Berlin was interested in this, because the Balkans was a political and military sideshow and Pavelic, the leader of this new Croatia, was not an equal partner.

As far as a politically convincing solution was concerned, the *Reich* fell short, but there remained Fascist Italy, which was less totalitarian than National Socialist Germany and which had not made racial hatred the doctrine of its state.

Italy made attempts to wage war, not only militarily but also to intensify its political maneuvering in order to introduce a new solution on a European level. This was especially true between the years 1942 to 1943. A "European Carta" should have guaranteed the prosperity, sovereignty and freedom of all nations under Axis control, but the National Socialists, committed to the ways of terror and unforgiveness, turned down this project. It is also doubtful if Rome would have been able to play the role of the honest mediator and find a just supranational settlement, because it considered the Balkans and especially the southern Slavic area as its own sphere of interest.

Without a uniting string, without an obligatory idea and without a strong central power, the southern Slavic area relapsed into the old, partly atavistic pattern of behavior. A kind of bloody and tribal warfare erupted with cruel excesses against other national or ethnic groups and wide spread banditry (you were not able to distinguish some partisan units from gangs of bandits).

In some parts of the country, a *"bellum omnium contra omnes"* raged and considerable areas were a deadly "no man's land." An important reason for this was that the various provinces had been influenced by different rules and occupiers and as a result, the southern Slavic area had never developed into a united land. Romans, Byzantines, Venetians, and Turks had ruled at different times, but had never been able to extinguish the various national aspirations for independence or fantasies of super power status.

Even in Macedonia, which was partitioned between Bulgaria, Greece, and Serbia, the dream of a Global Empire of Alexander the Great was still very much alive. Irredentism, chauvinism, religious and ideological hatred, all formed the breeding ground of the tragedy in Yugoslavia. The German intervention was only the beginning of a much bigger war, which in reality was composed of civil wars, national wars of liberation, wars of conquest, religious wars and wars of extermination.

The radical Croat Ustashe movement's unwillingness to forgive the Serbs was a decisive reason for the brutality of the conflict. The Ustashe used deportation, forced baptism, and terror against Serbs. Whole villages were razed. The massacres assumed such proportions that even the German occupation government protested. The concentration camps in Croatia became real killing fields. Jasenovac being the most notorious.[2]

After the war the Communist propaganda took hold of this subject and maintained that between 700,000 and 1,500,000 people, most of them Serbs, had been killed in Jasenovac alone. The Serbian Titoists tried to prove the "Genocidal nature" of the Croatian people with this false information.

---

[2] According to the author, Ekkehard Voelkl, ("Abrechnungsfuror in Kroatien" in Politische Saeuberung in Europa: Die Abrechnung mit Faschismus und Kollaboration nach dem Zweiten Weltkrieg" Deutscher Taschenbuch Verlag: Muenchen, 1991. Page 361.- the Editor

Impartial research has now revealed that the number of victims in Jasenovac amounted to between 60-80,000 people. The Serbs response to the Ustashe brutality was counter terror. Their actions far exceeded the legitimate defensive actions and were also directed against the noninvolved Muslims, who were slaughtered in the thousands. The old hatred against the century-long Turkish occupation resurfaced once again.

The Communist Partisans, who became the strongest force in Yugoslavia at the end of the war, finally murdered because of ideological reasons. Their targets were the political opponents, the class enemy, the occupation troops.

Yugoslavia became a slaughterhouse. The eyewitness, Fitzroy Maclean, a British officer, described the tortured country as a place *"of burning villages, desecrated churches, massacred hostages, and, mutilated bodies."* The tactic of the occupation forces to react with mass executions to the Communist and Monarchist guerrilla movements further escalated the situation. The Axis troops were numerically too weak to "pacify" the southern Slavic area and therefore soon fell back to relying on indigenous forces.

Montenegrin and Serbian volunteer corps, ethnic German units, a Czarist corps, Croatian divisions of the *Wehrmacht* (German Armed Forces), and Bosnian divisions of the Waffen-SS came into existence. No other theater of operations in World War II saw a similar great number of foreign units fighting side by side with the Germans. The motives of the Serbian, Croatian, Slovenian, Bosnian, Montenegrin, and Macedonian volunteers were manifold as were their different uniforms which they wore. The least of them were National Socialists. Most of them fought for the autonomy or national liberty of their region and against Communism, but often with sympathy for the western Allies.

After extensive source study, Antonio J. Munoz has described these events, this kaleidoscope of heroism and treason, rivalry and intrigue in detail with knowledge, fairly and - if this is possible at all - outlined it with great objectivity. It is good that an American author has written about this subject. Not only because of the physical distance separating him from the region in question, but also because Americans have been entangled in the Balkan troubles of this century far less than Europeans, and this is a decisive requirement for an unprejudiced description and appraisal of the southern Slavic tragedy.

After September 1943 matters became more dramatic and complicated, when Italy changed sides. Now Italians fought each other in the Balkans - followers of Mussolini, allied with the Germans, against the remains of the Italian occupation forces, which had sided with the Partisans (the same Partisans who had territorial claims against Venetia, Giulia, and Triest[3]).

Remnants of the *Regia Aeronautica*, Badoglio's co-belligerent air force, made supply drops for Tito, who reached out for Italian territory and Carinthia. But it also started fomenting trouble within the Axis forces. The relationship between Benito Mussolini's new *Republica Sociale Italiane* and the Independent State of Croatia reached an absolute low, because of Croatian territorial claims in Istria and Dalmatia. The *Duce* didn't even send an ambassador to Zagreb.

To add to the confusion, new combatants entered the Yugoslav theater in the beginning of 1943. These were General Helmuth von Pannwitz's Cossacks - allied to the Germans and fanatical anti-Communists. The likewise anti-Communist Slovenian Home Guard (Slovensko Domobranstvo), which comprised the core of the Slovenian Catholic youth, came into existence in the recently established *"Operationszone Adriatisches Kustenland"* (Zone of Operations Adriatic Coast), under Nazi Party Leader [Dr. Alois] Friedrich Rainer. This formation also had strong sympathies for the western Allies - but these didn't land in

---

[3] All Italian owned - the Editor.

Yugoslavia, neither in Montenegro nor in Dalmatia or Istria.

Winston Churchill's attitude towards Yugoslavia was especially ambiguous. On the one hand he left the country to Stalin, because he had conceded to limit British influence in postwar Yugoslavia to 10%. On the other hand he tried to persuade US president Roosevelt into landing in the Balkans. When he didn't succeed in this he tried everything to snatch the Dodecanese islands, especially Rhodes, during the Italian collapse in 1943, to win over Turkey. Turkey should have conquered the Balkans before the Soviets entered that area, and in this way could have secured it for the west.

But the German Armed Forces foiled the Allied takeover of the Dodecanese, although it had to fight six fold superior forces. Until 1945 Churchill did nothing to oppose Communism in Yugoslavia's domestic policy. He was only interested in who had killed more Germans - the Chetniks or the Communists under Tito. Churchill cut off his support for the pro-western Chetnik leader Draza Mihailovich, when the Communists proved to be more effective in this respect.

British support for Tito and Stalin reached its climax in April/May 1945, when the British turned over to their mortal enemies by trickery and force the tens of thousands of Cossacks, Croats, Slovenians, Serbs and Montenegrins who had fought on the German side.

Communist Yugoslavia, which was initially based on terror, didn't last half a century. Today after the international community's diplomatic recognition of Slovenia and Croatia, which was enforced by Vienna and Bonn/Berlin, the Balkans is once again aflame. The chauvinistic theory of a "Greater Serbia," being one of the initiating factors that caused World War I, now covers Bosnia-Herzegovina with violence and terror.

The Serbian aggression is a war against central Europe. The starting point is nearly the same as it was in 1914: Vienna and Bonn/Berlin sympathizing with the unfortunate Bosnia-Herzegovina, whereas London, Paris and Russia side with Serbia - even though not always as frankly.

Yugoslavia, being an artificial product of Allied diplomacy, has brought its inhabitants no lasting luck. Hatred rules again and the idea of a federation of nations, religions and races with equal rights is only a chimera again. A supranational and acceptable idea, a writing consensus, which guarantees cultural and ethnic diversity, is lacking. The words Leo Valiane wrote for the Italian daily, *Corriere della Sera* on May 24th, 1980 are still valid: *"Austria-Hungary is irrevocably gone and nobody strives for its restoration, but until today the vacuum it has left behind has not been filled out."*

Hans Werner Neulen
Cologne, in December, 1994

11

Indigenous Axis Forces in Yugoslavia

It was only during the Second World War that the use of guerrilla warfare was introduced on a truly grand scale and recognized as a means by which a country which had been defeated in the conventional manner, could continue an armed struggle against the victorious enemy army and its governing apparatus.

The Allies all across Europe and even in the Pacific practiced this style of unconventional warfare. This was especially true in the Soviet Union and the Balkans (Yugoslavia, Albania, and Greece), where guerrilla warfare was not only the most intense in all of Europe, but was fought in a cruel, savage and uncompromising manner by all parties involved.

This type of irregular warfare threatened the rear areas and lines of communications of the Axis forces, principally Nazi Germany. The German response was to bolster its defenses and garrisons by bringing into these threatened areas more troops. This was the desired effect that the Allies wished - to deflect Axis strength from the main battlefronts in North Africa or the Soviet Union (and later, to Italy in 1943 and France in 1944).

As time wore on, this reinforcement of garrison forces became much more difficult, since the Germans were less and less able to afford this due to heavy losses on the main battlefronts. In addition, almost from the very beginning of the occupation, the Germans had made a conscience effort to limit the number of forces which they would place in the Balkans as garrison troops. This would later change in 1943 when Italy's pullout from the war created a great power vacuum in that region - thus necessitating the transfer of substantial German forces from other theaters of operations.

Thus, up until the middle of 1943, German occupation policy included the use of the barest minimum number of forces occupying the countryside. Whether this was a wise course of action or not has been very hotly contested, but this lack of sufficient troops to deal with an occupation which obviously required more forces was to directly affect the rise of the collaborationist, indigenous Axis forces. Because there was a need to control these occupied countries, and no forces were either available or earmarked for the Balkans, the Germans (and Italians) came up with the idea of recruiting locally raised volunteer formations to help bolster their control in that region of Europe.

The formula was one which had been practiced in other parts of Europe and the Soviet Union. Elements of the population sympathetic to the Axis cause were to be exploited for troops. As time wore on, the Germans would even resort to drafting men into their collaborationist formations (with mixed results). This conscription of the local population produced (for the most part) mediocre to poor results, but shows how desperate they were to augment their meager forces.

This policy of recruiting locally raised full time and auxiliary formations became prevalent when the Germans finally realized that they didn't possess sufficient forces to garrison the former Yugoslavia with the forces available (including their Italian, Hungarian, and Bulgarian Axis allies). The very rugged-ness of the terrain made it very easy to hide and employ a guerrilla army, while at the same time, it made it very difficult for a conventional garrison force (and a weak one at that) to hunt down and destroy those same guerrillas.

The benefits of having a "homespun" collaborationist force in the Balkans was immediate. These not only included the propaganda benefits, but also took into account the fact that these native volunteers (1) knew the land, and (2) knew its people. Supported by these volunteer units, the Germans and their Axis allies were able to counter the growing guerrilla menace much more effectively. An additional advantage was that these locally raised units knew the local language and customs, and would (in theory) benefit the occupation army in their relationship with the subjugated populace.

Finally, having a native military force, with a puppet government to back up their actions and give these forces an air of legal authority, the Axis powers could claim that they were acting on behalf of these local "governments" and could thus label the guerrillas as "bandits." In fact, the German command did not begin to refer to the Tito or Chetnik guerrillas as military formations until 1943. Up until then, they had been referred to as "bandit groups" or simply as "highwaymen."

Finally, the raising of various militias and private armies under Italian, Hungarian, Bulgarian, or German auspices allowed the existing political, ethnic/racial, and religious hatreds among the equally diverse peoples that made up Yugoslavia, to boil over much faster than they would have. That Yugoslavia was an artificial entity there is no question. It was the product of the Treaty of Versailles and was doomed to split and fragment, as it inevitably did in 1991. In fact, tensions were already extremely high in Yugoslavia by the time of the Nazi occupation. The Axis invasion simply accelerated Yugoslavia's downward spiral to violence and fragmentation.

The Germans and their Axis allies then, are guilty of having exacerbated the situation by taking advantage of the various ethnic, political, territorial, and religious differences. That being said however, It should also be pointed out that these hatreds existed between these various peoples long before any Axis soldier crossed the Yugoslav border. Hitler wanted Yugoslavia to be another Axis partner. He had no territorial claims there. The pro-British *coup d'etat* on March 27th created a dangerous position for Nazi Germany, who was in the midst of making preparations to invade the Soviet Union. Hitler needed a stable southern front and an aggressive Yugoslavia threatened that stability. This is why Hitler invaded that country.

The invasion of Yugoslavia and the subsequent Royalist Chetnik and Communist guerrilla movements led to the creation of these native Axis units and militias. The Germans allowed a Serbian puppet government (headed by General Milan Nedic) to organize the Serbian State & Frontier Guard, which reached a peak strength of some 20,000 men by the summer of 1942.[4] In addition, the Serbian nationalist *"Zbor"* ("Rally") movement under Dimitrije Ljotic was allowed to organize a volunteer formation (which eventually numbered some 12,000 men) and became known as the Serbian Volunteer Corps. This unit was considered by the Germans as the most effective native, anti-Communist formation which served the Axis cause during the war.

The Germans also organized the ethnic German population in Yugoslavia. In northern Slovenia, they raised the *"Volkdeutsche Wehrmannschaft"* with three, then later five battalions. In Serbia they used ethnic-German Serbs to help form the *"Hilfspolizei"* (auxiliary police), although mercenaries and foreign adventurers also served in this notorious organization. In 1942 an ethnic German Serbian SS division (the "Prinz Eugen") was raised in the Banat region, but the Germans had to resort to conscription to fully man the 15,000+ unit. It performed effectively and even gained a brutal reputation.

The Bulgarians organized various militia battalions in Macedonia, mainly from the members of IMRO (the Inner Macedonian Revolutionary Organization), who had sought independence for Macedonia from Yugoslavia. The Hungarians drafted men from the Backa region into their army, while the Italians formed the MVAC, or *"Milizia Voluntare Anti Communista"* (Anti Communist Volunteer Militia). In Slovenia, the Catholic community

---

[4] "For Croatia And Christ: The Croatian Army, 1941-45" by Antonio J. Munoz. In <u>Axis Europa</u> magazine: Bayside, January 1995. Volume I, Number I, page 3.

was approached in order to help form units for the MVAC. This was also done in Dalmatia and other parts of Yugoslavia and Albania. In many cases, the Italians even armed the local (anti-Communist) Royalist Chetnik forces and absorbed them into their MVAC!

In Slovenia, the "White Guard" (as they were referred to by the Slovenian Communists) had been set up into two distinct categories: (1) the *"Vaske Straze"* ("Village Guards"), and the (2) *"Legiya Smrti"* ("Legion of Death"). The "Village Guards" were Catholic farmers and villagers who had been armed by the Italians and formed into defense militias which were static units, organized for the defense of their local town, village, or region. They had no special uniform and usually only wore civilian clothing with a bandoleer and rifle. Their function was to defend against partisan raiding parties.

The *"Legiya Smrti"* ("Legion of Death") was formed using unmarried men who did not have a crop to harvest, and therefore were ready for action at a moments' notice and could operate outside of their native region. These men were also Catholics and supported the Vatican in Rome. As such, they were ardent anti-Communists who were prepared to cooperate with the Italian occupation army. There was also a small force of some 1,600 Chetnik (Royalist) troops in Slovenia who were loyal to Draza Mihailovich and the exiled King Peter II in England. These were referred to by the Slovenian Communists as the "Blues" and were split up into two "brigades" (actually battalions in strength) named the 1st "Triglav", and 2nd "Krim" Brigades (more on these units later).

When Italy withdrew from the war in September, 1943 the Germans assumed responsibility for all Italian-sponsored Yugoslav collaborationist forces. This included the Slovenian "White Guard" and renamed them as the *"Slovenski Domobranci"* (Slovene Home Guard). In 1944, another Slovenian pro-Axis formation also came into existence, this time for use on the Istrian peninsula, and in the Italian province of Fiume.

This was titled the *"Slovenski Narodni Varnostni"* ("Slovenian National Security Force), which operated in the Slovenian Littoral. It never exceeded more than 2,000 men.

Slovenian Axis Forces in Italian Service, 1941-1943

In April, 1941 when Yugoslavia was conquered, the invading Axis forces set about occupying the countryside and carving up the the defeated nation into their spheres of influence. In Slovenia, the Italians occupied & annexed the Primorska region and part of the Notranjska area as well (please see the map on the next page), incorporating as a part of their "Fiume" province. The Slovenian capital of Ljubljana and its surrounding countryside, along with the Dolenjska and Bela Krajina regions were all merged together and renamed as the *"Provincia Lubiana"* ((Ljubljana Province). This region was not annexed, but was occupied. To the north, the province of Gorenjska became *"Oberkrain"* (Upper Carnolia), while the Koroska and Stajerska regions were merged and renamed *"Untersteiermark"* (Lower Styria). These two newly created provinces were annexed by Germany and duly occupied.

In April, 1941 Dr. Marko Natlacen, who before the war headed the Catholic Slovene People's Party, formed the National Committee for an Independent Slovenia. Dr. Natlacen had formed a "Slovenian Legion" during the Axis invasion which aided in disarming defeated units of the Yugoslav army. Slovenian nationalist Catholic elements hoped that the breakup of Yugoslavia might lead to Slovenian independence, but they were to be disappointed. The Germans and Italians divided the country between themselves and left the eastern tip to be occupied by the Hungarians.

ganize a *"Chetnik"* force in Slovenia from the Serbian minority there. The Chetniks were (almost exclusively) Serbian guerrillas who backed the exiled King of Yugoslavia (who was also a Serb). The Chetniks hated the predominantly Communist partisans (the feeling was mutual). Although they were organized to fight the Axis occupation, the ani-

In spite of this apparent lack of independence, the *"Slovenska Legiya"* (Slovene Legion) continued to serve, now under Italian service as auxiliary troops.

In November, 1941 Ernst Peterlin (with Italian army permission) organized another pro-Axis militia from the local Slovene (Catholic) farmers in the regions annexed and occupied by Italy. Peterlin's militia was a static, self-defense organization whose purpose was to deny the growing partisan movement the ability to gather foodstuffs and to recruit young men from the local farms, villages, and towns. This was done by forming militia companies whose volunteers were farmers but who could be called on to defend their local areas from guerrilla incursions.

These static, self-defense companies were named after the local town or village in each area where they were raised. Initially, these *"Vraske Straze"* (Village Guards) numbered some 1,000 men. Since the farmers were tied down to the crops, their employment was quite limited and static in nature.

In July, 1941 Royalist Major Novak helped or-

BELOW: How Slovenia Was Divided Between the Axis Forces

mosity which was felt by both of these groups eventually led to armed conflict between them.

15

On August 6th, 1942 the Italians officially absorbed the Village Guard into their MVAC, or "Milizia Voluntare Anti-Communista" (Anti-Communist Volunteer Militia). Ernest (Ernst) Peterlin was given the rank of Lieutenant-Colonel in the MVAC. The clothing of these Slovenian volunteers changed dramatically in 1942 with the introduction of black berets, on which a metallic sword & shield emblem was pinned. On the side of the beret, the men wore the standard MVAC rank insignia. This insignia was in the form of a triangular cloth in various colors to denote rank.

In the case of platoon, company, and battalion commanders, a five-pointed tin star was pinned to this triangular cloth emblem.

The rank structure was as follows:

Red cloth triangle - Squad Sub-Commander
Red cloth triangle
& white *cloth* star - Squad Commander
Yellow cloth triangle - Platoon Sub-Commander
Yellow cloth triangle
& tin star - Platoon Commander
Silver cloth triangle - Company Sub-Commander
Silver cloth triangle
& tin star - Company Commander
Gold cloth triangle - Battalion Sub-Commander
Gold cloth triangle & tin star - Battalion Commander

By December, 1942 there were around 4,500 Village Guards divided into 41 MVAC companies which were in turn, located in 71 stationary posts. By July, 1943 these numbers had risen to 6,000 men in 107 posts.

In March, 1942 the outlawed Slovene political parties formed the "Slovene National Alliance." These various national groups were basically pro-western and anti-Communist but were willing to cooperate with the occupation forces for the sake of eliminating the Communist partisans. The Slovene National Alliance merged with the "Slovene Legion" of Dr. Natlacen. This alliance also included the prewar Catholic Action movement and another conservative group, the *"Narodna Legija"* (National Legion). All of these groups considered themselves allied to Draza Mihailovic's Royalist Chetniks (even though almost all of its members were Catholic and not Eastern Orthodox Christians.

In September, 1942 most of these men were largely absorbed into the Italian-sponsored MVAC, leaving around 3-4,000 men to be organized in early 1943 into four (Slovenian) "Chetnik" detachments. These four detachments were eventually referred to by the Communist partisans as the *"Plava Garda"* (Blue Guard) in order to differentiate them from the Village Guard, which they now called the "White Guard."

A month earlier, in August, 1942 Major Novak's Royalist Chetnik force of 640 men was absorbed into the Italian MVAC and re-titled the *"Legija smrti"* (Legion of Death). With Italian backing, this force was greatly expanded using volunteers from the Slovenian Catholic National Alliance. These volunteers were almost exclusively unmarried, young men, who were not tied down to the land, and could therefore be employed at any time and at any place. The unit quickly developed a tough reputation that preceded them anywhere they went.

By February, 1943 the Legion of Death had been expanded to 11 companies totaling 1,687 men. These eleven companies were split up into three (3) battalions whose home bases were as follows:

Ist Battalion/ Legion of Death - Vrnika
IInd Battalion/ Legion of Death - Gorjanci
IIIrd Battalion/ Legion of Death - Mokronag

In July, 1943 the Slovene National Alliance came to the conclusion that their forces, employing basically static defense tactics (with the exception of the mobile Legion of Death), were losing the war against the highly mobile and hit and run tactics of the Communist partisans. They thus began to reorganize their forces into what was a planned 19-battalion force. Still considered part of the MVAC, it was to be called the *"Slovenska Narodna Vojska"* (Slovene National Army).

In July, 1943 Sicily had been invaded by the Allies and rumors were ripe about a possible Allied landing on the Yugoslavian coastline. The Slovenian nationalists welcomed this prospect and even developed a plan to immediately switch sides should such an Allied landing take place, but the anticipated invasion never materialized and the plan was never completed.

When the Italian surrender occurred in September, 1943 Captain Albin Cerkvenik organized 1,600 former Slovenian MVAC men and 60 Serbian Chetniks into two Slovenian "Chetnik" units and declared them anti-Communist & pro-Mihailovic. He gave them the grandiose title of the "Slovene Chetnik Army," even though the strength of each of its only two "brigades" was an average of 800 men apiece. The 1st Brigade was named *"Triglav,"* while its 2nd Brigade was titled *"Krim."*

As stated, Italy surrendered on September 8th, 1943. The Slovenian partisans seized on this opportunity to arm themselves with Italian mi-

litary equipment by moving to disarm as many Italian units on Slovenian soil as they could reach. The Slovenian nationalist (and Chetnik) forces tried to do this as well, but the Partisans were able to argue with the Italians that they were the true representatives of the Allied side, and as a result, the only ones that should receive the surrender of Italian units. This argument won out in most cases, and as a result, the small Slovene partisan force received a large influx of weapons, especially heavy arms such as mortars, artillery pieces, and tanks.

Now armed with tanks, artillery, and other heavy weapons, as well as an ample supply of munitions and small arms, the 3,000 man partisan force in Slovenia set out to destroy their nationalist opponents. It was the partisan *"Presen"* Brigade which caught Cerkvenik's 1,600 man "army" still in the process of forming at Turjak Castle (about 20 kilometers south-southeast of the capital of Ljubljana). The mainly White Guard units there were quickly surrounded and a siege followed.

The partisans, armed with numerous artillery pieces, pounded the castle with artillery rounds and promises of leniency if the nationalists would surrender. The siege ended on September 19th, 1943 with the almost complete annihilation of both nationalist brigades. The Blue Guard were also handed a devastating defeat that month in the area of Kocevje. After this defeat, "Chetnik" forces in Slovenia would never amount to more than 500 men. The only unit which remained undefeated during this time was the Legion of Death, whose battalions fought with great tenacity.

Throughout the Slovenian countryside, partisan units began to overrun MVAC outposts. All White Guard and Blue Guard units which could escape, headed for the protection of German controlled areas, like the capital, Ljubljana, where its former mayor, Leon Rupnik, was trying to reorganize a new Slovenian collaborationist force under German auspices.

Slovenian Axis Forces in German Service, 1943-1945

On September 10th, 1943 - just two days after the Italian surrender, the Germans attached the former *"Provincia di Lubiana"* (Ljubljana Province) to their newly created *"Operationszone Adriatisches Kuestenland"* (Operational Zone - Adriatic Coast). This was the military district created by the *Wehrmacht* (German Armed Forces) for administrative and operational control of this northeastern region of Italy as well as western and central areas of Slovenia. In addition, the SS command created the *"Hoeheren SS und Polizeifuehrer Adriatisches Kuestenland"* (Higher SS & Police Leader Adriatic Coast). This SS position was given to SS Major General and Lieutenant General of the Police Odilo Globocnik.

On September 24th, 1943 Leon Rupnik (who had also been an ex-Lieutenant-General in the Yugoslav army) organized the *"Slovenska Domobranska Legija"* (Slovene Defense Legion) from 2,000 former MVAC men. This legion was quickly organized into three combat battalions. Six days later, on September 30th, the Germans assumed control of this force and quickly renamed the force as the *"Slovenski Domobranci"* (Slovene Home Guard).

Although Leon Rupnik retained his rank of Lieutenant-General, he was nevertheless relegated to running the civilian collaborationist government in Ljubljana, while an ethnic-German named Franc Krenner, was given the rank of colonel and assigned actual operational control over the Slovenian Home Guard. Rupnik was given the title of "Inspector General of the Home Guard," but it was only a figurehead position. Actual operational control over the Slovenian Home Guard was given to Colonel Franc Krener, a pudgy and balding middle-aged ethnic-German Slovene. Leon Rupnik's son, Vuk Rupnik was also a top officer in the Home Guard. He was a major and later was promoted to colonel. In January, 1945 he was awarded the German Iron Cross (1st Class) for leading a battalion of the Home Guard in battle.

This initial Home Guard force of 2,000 men was quickly expanded to 63 companies, of which 43 companies were distributed throughout the Slovenian countryside as small garrison outposts, while the remainder were grouped into battalions [please see page 19 for a list of these units and their postings]. The uniform was now changed and the Germans supplied a grey-green blouse and accompanying trouser. This grey-green uniform might have come from ex-Dutch army stocks, although there is ample photographic evidence that German police uniforms were also distributed.

In many cases (especially during the second half of 1943), the old Italian brown colored uniforms (light brown, or tan for officers) was still used, but by the summer of 1944 the Home Guard units were dressed in either grey-green or German police uniforms which were more of a darker green-grey color. Boots used were either of Italian or German origin. The helmets were ex-Italian army, while the soft covers were mainly German police style.

The Slovenian national eagle was introduced as a cloth insignia in blue against a white background shield. This was worn on the left sleeve. In addition, the Italian helmets were decorated with a painted shield showing the Slovenian national colors of white, blue, & red. This shield was painted on the side of the helmets. The shoulder boards were typical German police insignia. The soft cover initially used the triangular metallic cockade with the Slovene national colors (white-blue-red), but later was changed to an oval cockade.

SLOVENE HOME GUARD COMPANIES / WINTER, 1943 - 1944

REGION	COMPANY	LOCATION	LOCATION	LOCATION	LOCATION
	1st	Brezovica			
N	2nd	Notranje gorice			
	3rd	Borovnica			
	4th	Borovnica			
	5th	Verd			
N	6th	Logated			
	7th	Rakek			
L, N	11th	Ljubljana	Rudnik	Smarje	
L	12th	Ljubljana			
	13th	Polje	Rakek		
	14th	Polje			
L	15th	Dravlje	Skofljica	Veliki	Gaber
	16th	Rudnik			
L, N	17th	Ljubljana	Vrhnika		
L	18th	Ljubljana			
	19th	Dobrova			
L	20th	Ljubljana			
	21st	Crna vas	Ig	Obcine	
L	22nd	Skofljica	Pijava gorica		
L	23rd	Skofljica			
D	24th	Velike lasce			
D	25th	Velike lasce	Ribnica		
D	26th	Velike lasce	Grosuplje	Visnja gora	
D	27th	Grosuplje			
	28th				
D	29th	Velike lasce			
D	31st	Novo mesto			
	32nd	Grm			
D	33rd	Novo mesto	Trebnje		
	34th	Locna			
	35th	Grm	Trzisce		
D	36th	Kostanjevica	Sv. Ana		
	37th	Lesnica			
	38th	Kandija			
D, L	39th	Novo mesto	Sentvid =	(St. Vid)	
	40th	Locna	Dolnji vrh		
N	41st	Vrhnika			
	42nd	Polhov gradec			
	43rd	St. Jost	Rorjul		
	44th	Rovte			
N	45th	Logatec			
	46th	Hotedrseica			
	47th				

REGION	COMPANY	LOCATION	LOCATION	LOCATION	LOCATION
	48th				
	51st	Bela cerkev			
	52nd				
D	53rd	Novo mesto			
D	54th	Novo mesto			
D	55th	Trebnje			
	56th				
D	61st	Kocevje			
D	62nd	Kocevje			
D, L, N	65th	Ribnica	Zdenska vas	Ljubljana	Vrhnika
L	66th	Ljubljana			
L	67th	Ljubljana			
	71st	Sticna			
N	72nd	Vrhnika			
N	111th	Dravlje	Rudnik		
N	112th	Rudnik	Vrhnika		
D	113th	Zgornja siska			
D	114th	Zgornja siska	Velike lasce		
D	115th	Zgornja siska	Ribnika		

KEY	REGION
L	Ljubljana
D	Dolenjska
N	Notranjska

NOTE: Those companies which were not stationed as garrison companies were formed into five infantry battalions with the intent of using them to help hunt down and destroy the Slovenian partisans. One of these five battalions became a training unit and was not employed in combat.

On September 30th, 1943 the Germans assumed control of the "Slovene Defense Legion," which had been formed just six days earlier (on September 24th) by Leon Rupnik. Of the 63 companies in existence by the beginning of 1944, 43 of them were spread out as garrisons, while the remaining twenty (20) companies were formed into combat battalions. There were special support companies that were also organized. An Engineers, Communications, Medical, and Contruction Company were also raised. The men of the Communications (Signals) Company wore a special metallic insignia on their collars. It resembled two lightning bolts crisscrossing one another [please see the photographic section of this book for a look at the only known surviving photograph of this special insignia]. Finally, three Slovene Home Guard artillery batteries were created using captured Italian guns. The 1st & 2nd Batteries were stationed in Ljubljana, while the 3rd Artillery Battery was located at Velike lasce.

BELOW: The metallic insignia worn on the collar by Home Guard communications troops.

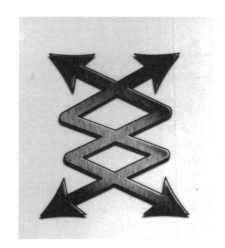

The formation of the five Slovene Home Guard combat battalions occurred between September - November 1943. By late September, 1943 three battalions were organized. A fourth battalion, complete with a training school was established in November. This training battalion and school was located in Ljubljana. A combat battalion was also organized in November, in the town of Novo Mesto, so by December 1st, 1943 the Home Guard could count on the following organzied battalions:

Home Guard Battalion	Home Station
1st Battalion	Ljubljana
2nd Battalion	Vrhnika
3rd Battalion	Kostanjevica
4th Battalion *	Ljubljana
5th Battalion	Novo Mesto

* This was a training battalion and was not normally employable in a combat role.

As soon as the Germans assumed control of the Slovene collaborationist units, they changed the title from *"Slovenska domobranska legija"* (Slovene Defense Legion) to *"Slovensko domobranstvo"* (Slovene Home Guard). The headquarters of the Home Guard was initially referred to as *"Inspektorat Slovenskaga domobranstva"* (Inspectorate of the Slovene Home Guard). This was, as stated earlier, supposed to be run by Lieutenant-General Leon Rupnik, but was actually administered by Colonel Franc Krenner. This headquarters was retitled on October 12th, 1943 as the *"Organizacijski stab Slovenskega domobranstva"* (Organization Staff of the Slovene Home Guard).

This Slovenian headquarters was in turn answerable to the XVIIIth SS Military District, whose main headquarters was located in Salzburg, Austria. The XVIIIth SS Military District and the post of Higher-SS & Police Leader "Alpenland" was headed by *SS Gruppenfuehrer und Generalleutnant der Wa-* *ffen-SS und Polizei* Erwin Roesner. Roesner's headquarters and his SS & police troops were responsible for combating the Slovene partisans.

The German civilian leader in charge of the Slovenian countryside was *SS-Obergruppen- ehrer* Dr. Alois Friedrich Rainer, the *"Gauleiter"* (District Leader") for Carinthia, and head of the civilian administration for the annexed Slovenian regions which the Germans called *"Oberkrain"* (Upper Krajina) and *"Untersteiermark"* (Lower Styria). In addition, Dr. Rainer was also given civilian control of what had been the Italian Fiume province and western Slovenia, including the former *"Provincia di Lubiana."* The Fiume province and the area of the Italo-Slovene border became known as the *"Adriatisches Kuestenland"* (Adriatic Coast Region). This region too, was assigned to Rainer's civilian control, but for guerrilla warfare purposes, was assigned to SS Major General & Lt. General of the Police Odilo Globocnic and the headquarters of "Higher SS & Police Leader Adriatic Coast."

On December 3rd, 1943 Dr. Alois Friedrich Rainer decreed that henceforth, all Slovenian males were to be made available for compulsory military service in the Slovene Home Guard. By the end of December 1943, the number of Slovenian men in the Home Guard reached 10,500. It was also in this month that the five Home Guard battalions were reorganized and expanded. From now on the battalions would be referred to as *"kampfgruppen"* (battlegroups), and their size would vary depending on the number of companies assigned at any one time.

One of these "kampfgruppen" was led by Major (then later, Colonel) Vuk Rupnik, Lt.Gen. Leon Rupnik's son. Vuk Rupnik would go on to receive the German Iron Cross (1st Class) in January, 1945 while leading a Home Guard battlegroup in combat. Major Rupnik was initially posted to the main headquarters of the Home Guard in *"Ljubljana Grad"* (Ljubljana Castle), which overlooks the city.

During the winter of 1943-44 the Home Guard battalions were reorganized and expanded to include seven battlegroups with varying numbers of companies. These combat groups were located in the following places:

Combat Group	Number of Companies	Location
1st	9 companies	Ljubljana
2nd	7 companies	Skofljica*
3rd	8 companies	Novo Mesto
4th	5 companies	Vrhnika
5th	6 companies	Borovnika
6th	2 companies	Kocevje**
7th	6 companies	Grosuplje***

In Ljubljana, the Home Guard School was reorganized into two school units: 1st School Unit and 2nd School Unit. The 2nd School Unit was abolished and disbanded on January 15th, 1944. At this time, three Home Guard artillery batteries were also set up using captured Italian guns. The batteries were numbered consecutively from 1-3 and were stationed as follows:

> 1st Home Guard Battery - Ljubljana
> 2nd Home Guard Battery - Lubljana
> 3rd Home Guard Battery - Velike Lasce

The month of February, 1944 saw a major reorganization take place in the Home Guard. The seven combat groups were disbanded and reformed into four larger combat groups called *"skupine"*. These new groups were numbered and identified as follows:

1st War (Training) Unit - This was the ex-1st Group. It contained nine (9) rifle companies, 6 training companies, one (1) engineer company, and two artillery batteries. This war unit was stationed in Ljubljana.

2nd War Unit - This was the railway security formation whose headquarters was organized officially on February 25th, 1944 in order to safeguard the Ljubljana - Rakek - Postojna - Ljubljana - Skofljika - Grosuplje rail line. In order to accomplish this, five armoured trains were supplied by the Germans, who also supplied the Order Police and Rail Police officers to command the Slovene Home Guard troopers, numbering twelve (12) companies in all. This war unit had been formed from the ex-4th & 5th (former) war units.

3rd War Unit - This formation was placed under the control of the Ist battalion/ 14th SS Police Regiment. This German Order Police regiment was operating in the upper Krajina region of northern Slovenia in the beginning of 1944. This war unit contained eleven (11) companies of Home Guards soldiers. They were charged with protecting the Novo mesto area. A special headquarters staff was organized to control these companies and was called the *Zeleznisko vanostno poveljstvo* (Railway Security Headquarters).

4th War Unit - This formation included troops who had formerly served in Skofljika, Velike Lasce, and Grosuplje. They had formed the ex-2nd, 6th, & 7th (former) war units. This war unit was directly under the control of the Slovene Home Guard Headquarters, but was also available for employment by any local or regional German military unit (police, army, or otherwise). This unit also included former soldiers from the "Kriz" Assault Battalion (formed in the fall of 1943).

This organization remained the same until mid-May, 1944 when the strength of the Slovene Home Guard had by then reached a strength of twelve thousand (12,000) men. After the initial success of the storm unit, the

Germans decided to expand on the concept by increasing the number of "storm" battalions from one to four (one under each of the four war units). The initial storm battalion, which had been formed on March 26th , 1944 had contained two rifle (later raised to three) and one heavy weapons company. This small but highly flexible and mobile establishment had proven effective in combating the Slovene partisan units.

On May 16th, 1944 the whole country was divided into four operational zones, and (as stated above), each contained one *Udarni* (assault) battalion. The assault battalions were now located as follows:

OPERATIONAL AREA	PROVINCE (note)[1]	BATTALION
Ljubljana	Ljubljana	"Nord"
Rakak	Notranjska	"West"
Grosuplje	Dolenjska	"Mitte"
Trebnje	Dolenjska	"Ost"

On July 5th, 1944 these storm battalions were numbered consecutively as follows:

DESIGNATION	STORM BATTALION
1st	"Nord"
2nd	"West"
3rd	"Mitte"
4th	"Ost"
5th[2]	Alarm Btln. "Schmitz"

By the middle of 1944 the Home Guard had increased dramatically. It could now count on 63 rifle companies, and one company each of (a) engineers, (b) communications (signals), (c) medical, and (d) construction. It also contained four artillery batteries: two (2) located in Ljubljana, one (1) at Velike Lasce, and one (1) permanently attached to the armored trains (of which there were five).

The "Nord" Home Guard Group used its six training companies to guard the capital of Ljubljana, while its nine rifle companies were responsible for patrolling the valley of the Krka River all the way to Zuzemberk in the Dolenjska district and the area up to the village of Moravce (to the north).

The "Mitte" Home Guard Group with its eleven rifle companies had the duty of guarding the Ribnica Valley in the Kocevska district and part of the Suha Krajina district. The "West" Home Guard Group was charged with protecting the Polhovgrajski, and Dolomiti hills in the Notranjska district. The "Ost" Home Guard Group was to patrol the Dolenjska district with Novo mesto and the Bela Krajina district.

These Home Guard "Assault" battalions were organized in the same manner as the German SS Police units. They included three rifle companies and one heavy weapons company, but being formed from native volunteers, were considered much more dangerous to the guerrillas.

Heavy battles began to take a toll on the Home Guard forces beginning in July, 1944. Tito would grant an amnesty later in the summer to all Yugoslav Axis forces who voluntarily laid down their arms or switched sides. It was apparent that the Axis were now on the losing end of the war, and many former Axis soldiers from Yugoslavia chose to either desert or defect. The morale of the Slovene nationalist forces had been affected when the western Allies had decided to make amphibious landings in the northern and southern French coast, avoiding the Balkans altogether, save for a few, small, token landings on some islands on the Adriatic and Aegean Sea.

Faced with the realization that they could not expect the western Allies to help them prevent the fall of Slovenia to eventual Communist domination, many Slovenian nationalists lost

---

[1] The operational area of the Slovene Home Guard was principaly in the Ljubljana, Dolenjska, and Notranjska provinces, since the upper regions of Slovenia (Gorenjska, or Oberkrain, and Stajerska, or Untersteiermark) had been annexed by the Germans and therefore, officially, no purely Slovenian units could operate there. The Germans employed purely German units there, in addition to the ethnic-German Wehrmannschaft Regiment (five battalions). The German police units employed there during the fall of 1943 had been principally SS Police Regiment 14 & 19.

[2] On September 10th, 1944 a new Home Guard formation was raised from the Slovene *Domobranci* who had been defending the towns of Velike Lasce, Ribnica and Kocevje (Dolenjska region).

hope and simply gave up the struggle, while the most fanatical and diehard continued to serve alongside the Germans in a last-ditch effort to prevent a Communist victory in Slovenia.

Yet, in spite of these desertions, the Germans were able to maintain at least 6 Slovene Home Guard combat battalions in the field, as late as March, 1945 (plus a score of other, independent companies). The Germans, who had known all along that the Slovenian nationalists were hoping to be saved by the western Allies, never quite fully trusted the Domobranci. This became truly evident in December, 1944 when the German command decided to cannibalize one SS police rifle company to each of the Home Guard battalions (with the exception of the 2nd Battalion) from the 14th & 17th SS Police Regiments, then operating in the country.[3] This was apparently done to "stiffen" the Home Guard and also to keep a closer eye on their activities.

Another, more telling incident, was a German document, dated "14 January, 1945" which described how on December 30th, 1944 the local SS & Police forces had to disarm the Home Guard garrison at Bistrica. From the report, it seems as though the entire formation was forced to enter Austria, escorted by the German SS Police.[4]

Other captured documents indicate that the Germans were attempting to split up their collaborationist Axis forces into smaller, more manageable groups, and mingling them, whenever possible, with German or more reliable Axis troops. For example, on June 20th, 1944, in the Triest region, the town of Aidussina (Adelsberg) was garrisoned by a 49-man *Wehrmannschaft "Selbstschutz"* (Self Defense) platoon, and 76 men and 1 officer of the SNVZ 5th Company (IInd Battalion).[5]

Another, earlier example was at San Luccia (Triest region as well), where in mid-April 1944 the garrison was composed of 100 Germans, 150 Italians, and 50 "Domobranci".[6] On January 7th, 1945 the garrison of Aidussina would change to 140 "White Guardists" (i.e.- SNVZ troops) and "Nedic" men (remnants of the Serbian State & Frontier Guard forces). Three days later that number would slightly increase to 160 by the arrival of a platoon of twenty additional "Nedic" troops.[7]

In logatec (about 26 kilometers east-northeast of Aidussina, another 60 "White Guardists" (again, SNVZ troops), and 80 "Nedic" men were quartered as of January 10th, 1945.[8] A later report about Axis strength in the town of Aidussina (Adelsberg), listed 1,800 Germans, 80 "White Guardists", and between 1,500-2,000 "Nedic" men. This same report listed an additional 50 "White Guardists" at Vipava (6 kilometers southeast of Aidussina), 1,200 "Nedic" men in Prestanek (6 kilometers southwest of Aidussina), and 5-6,000 Axis troops (mixed German, Italian, Slovene) in Gorizia (Gorz). These and other reports prove that the Germans were trying to stiffen the resolve of the Home Guard by mixing their forces with German or other Axis units.

The existence of Slovenian Home Guard regiments has been denied by postwar Slovenian Communist forces. This seems rather self serving, since it implies that the Germans didn't trust the Domobranci enough to allow them to form regimental sized units, but what they fail to see is that by 1945 the Germans were in desperate straits, so much so that it would have been of little importance to the German command if Slovenian units were grouped into larger formations, so long as they were able to operate more effectively.

---

[3] The SS police regiments used may have been the 14th & 25th SS Police Regiments, although postwar Slovenian sources state that it was the 14th & 17th SS police regiments.

[4] NARS Microfilm T-501, Roll 261, Frame 000547.

[5] Kaltenegger, Roland. "Operationszone 'Adriatisches Kuestenland'. Der Kampf um Triest, Istrien und Fiume 1944/45". Leopold Stocker Verlag: Graz-Stuttgart, 1993. Page 124.

[6] ibid, page 77.

[7] NARS Microfilm T-501, Roll 266, Frame 000518.

[8] ibid, Frame 000539.

The first hint of these Domobranci regiments comes from a German *"Kriegsgliederung"* schematic report dated March 6th, 1945. Among numerous anti-partisan forces under the various SS & Police commands in Italy, the Austrian frontier and Slovenia, it lists (very clearly) three Domobranci "Assault" regiments and 30 Domobranci "defense" companies. Each regiment was carefully drawn, complete with two battalions of Home Guard troops apiece.

According to postwar Slovenian sources, as of March 28th, 1945 the Home Guard still contained the following battalions:

hoping to get Allied protection from the Tito forces.[10]

A day later, on May 4th it revived the "Slovene National Army" which had been planned in July 1943 (see box on page 26) but had petered out due to a lack of an Allied response. This new "Slovene National Army", composed of the remnants of the Slovene Home Guard, SNVZ, and the Carnolian Home Defense Forces (more on this unit later), might have decided to organize itself into four Home Guard regiments, but developments were moving too fast for them to have had time to organize these various forces

WHEN RAISED?	OLD DESIGNATION	NEW DESIGNATION
1944	1st Battalion	1st Battalion
1944	2nd Battalion	5th battalion
1944	3rd Battalion	DISBANDED March, 1945
July, 1944	4th Battalion	2nd Battalion
September, 1944	5th Battalion	6th Battalion
March, 1945	6th Battalion	10th Battalion
March, 1945	NEW	12th Battalion

The fact that these six battalions were still in existence at a time when the three Home Guard regiments were supposed to have contained altogether six battalions, leads one to conclude that indeed it was possible that the Germans may have authorized the formation of these regiments. In addition, one published source, written by a former Home Guard officer, mentions that the "1st", "2nd", "3rd", and even a "4th Home Guard Regiment" were in existence and had surrendered to British forces in May, 1945 at Blieburg, just inside the Austrian border.[9]

We know that on May 3rd, 1945 the Slovene National Alliance- that is, those nationalist forces that were against a Communist victory in Slovenia, proclaimed Slovenian "independence,"

into four regiments in less than a month. In addition, notice that of the 60+ companies that existed in 1944, 30 remained independent as of March, 1945. This leads us to consider that the other 30 were either disbanded, or formed into battalions and (yes) even possibly regiments. It is more likely therefore, that these regiments (at least three that we can cross-reference for sure) did in fact exist. German records prove it. Published Domobranci memoirs corroborate it, and circumstantial evidence points to it. As to the fate of the Slovene forces upon their surrender, it is fully documented on pages 64-65 of this book, but the short story is that they surrendered at Blieburg with the bulk of the Croatian Army, only

---

[9] Klepec, Matjaz. "Tuechern ist getraenkt mit unserem Blut: Das Schicksal der Heimwehrmaenner (Domobranci)". Editorial Baraga, SRL: Buenos Aires, 1973. Page 50.

[10] This in spite of the fact that many Slovenians, conscripted by the Italians to fight in North Africa, had been recruited by the Allies and had formed part of King Petar II's Royal Yugoslav Forces in Egypt.

to be handed back by the British to the Yugoslav Communists.

SLOVENES UNDER GESTAPO AUSPICES

On January 9th, 1944 the *Gestapo*, or *Geheimstaatspolizei* (State Secret Police) formed about 1,000 Slovenian volunteers from the annexed province of Upper Carnolia (*Oberkrain*). This was the former Slovene province of *Gorenjsko*. Previously only ethnic Germans had been allowed to form armed units in this province and in the province of *Untersteiermark* (or *Stajerska*). But the necessities of war had softened the attitude of the Germans.

The force was assigned a nominal Slovenian commander, who was initially Slavko Krek, but when he was killed, that title went to Franc Erpic. In reality, it was led and organized by what appears to have been a charismatic Austrian Gestapo sergeant named Erich Dichtl, who also had the ability of speaking the local language fluently.

The force was dubbed the *"Gorenjsko Domobranstvo"* (the "Upper Carnolia Defense Force"), but in the German language this title translates to *"Oberkrainer Selbstschutz"*, so it was also referred to by this name. The headquarters of the *"Oberkrainer Selbstschutz"* was in the city of Kranj (Krainburg). Sergeant Dichtl was methodical in his planning and by the end of 1944 he had enlarged his command to include 20 fortified towns and hamlets, with about 100 men apiece. In October, 1944 he gathered 100-150 of the best of these 2,000 volunteers into a special Gestapo assault company, whose mission was to hunt the guerrillas.

The Slovene National Army

From the very beginning, the majority of the collaborationist Slovene forces, both in Italian and then later, in German service were more concerned with keeping Slovenia (1) independent from the rest of Yugoslavia, and (2) free of Communist control. Their attitude towards the Axis occupation forces was that they were the lesser of two evils.

Many ethnic groups within the equally ethnically diverse Yugoslavia chose this old Arab approach to war which reads *"the enemy of my enemy is my friend."* It was in this way that the Slovenian nationalists found themselves Allied to the losing side of World War II.

In July, 1943 the Slovenian nationalists began a plan to use the existing Slovene forces under the Italian MVAC (Volunteer Anti-Communist Militia) to form a 19-battalion strong Slovene National Army *("Slovenska Narodna Vojska")* Their plan was to use this force to help support an expected Allied landing on the Adriatic coast. A landing which would herald the arrival of American and British forces that would not only expel the Germans but keep the Communists from seizing the countryside.

To the Dr. Natlacen, and all of the other independence minded nationalist leaders in Slovenia, it was impossible to imagine that England and America would leave the Balkans to Tito and his Communist supporters in Moscow. Yet, the expected landings only proved to be a deception from the real landings in Sicily and later, on the mainland of Italy itself.

On September 8th, 1943 the Italians, egged on by the King, some generals, and a war-weary nation, crumbled and sued for peace. Once again the nationalists sought to take advantage of the situation by forming a truly independent Slovenian nationalist force which could declare Slovenia's independence, but the Slovene (Communist) partisans reacted swiftly and destroyed most of the forces that had been quickly raised by Captain Albin Cerkvenik. His 1st "Triglav" and 2nd "Krim" Brigades, totalling some 1,600 former MVAC troops, were surprised at Turjak and destroyed, while the Slovenian Chetnik "Blue Guard" were virtually annihilated at Kocevje.

After this defeat, only 4-500 Slovene "Chetniks" operated in the countryside. Thereupon the Partisans turned their attention to eliminating as many White and Blue Guard posts as they could find. What nationalist forces that managed to escape the debacle at Turjak, Kocevje, and lesser disasters all went streaming towards the protection of German formations.

The nationalists now had no choice but to ally themselves with the Germans. The specter of a possible Allied landing on the Adriatic coast reared its tempting head once again, in the summer of 1944, but as before, it only proved a smoke screen for the Allied landings in northern and southern France. The declaration of a Slovene National Army on May 4th, 1945 was but a last-ditch attempt by these same pro-western, anti-Communist elements in Slovenia to remain free of Tito's control. It failed, like all of the other plans to obtain western sympathy and support.

Dichtl's force proved to be quite effective, so much so that by May, 1945 it had been enlarged to 2,600 men with 46 fortified posts. This force was designated as one of the three "divisions" of the stillborn Slovene National Army, which was declared in existence on May 4th, 1945. It is very fascinating to speculate how a *Gestapo* led, trained, and equipped force could have been considered a part of this pro-western "Slovene National Army," but it didn't seem to dawn on the nationalists that perhaps the western Allies might have second (or third) thoughts about accepting into their "protection" a unit that had been formed by such a blatantly Nazi organization as the *Gestapo*.

THE ETHNIC GERMAN *WEHRMANNSCHAFT*

Immediately after the defeat of Yugoslavia, the northern provinces of Slovenia, *Gorenjska* and *Stajerska*, and the small *Koroska* (see map on page 15) were incorporated into the *Reich* as the *Oberkrain* and *Untersteiermark* regions. In keeping with Nazi social and political practice, the ethnic German communities in these former Slovene provinces were organized into a paramilitary association known as the *Heimatbund*, which was supposed to represent the interests of these ethnic Germans, but was basically a means by which the Nazi Party could exert its influence on the ethnic population.

Shortly thereafter, the first militarized unit was raised from the most physically fit members of the *Heimatbund*, and was called the *Wehrmannschaft* (Defense Militia). The *Wehrmannschaft* came into being in the fall of 1941 and was trained mainly by the *SA*, or *Sturmabteilung* (storm troops, the Nazi Party's street soldiers). The *SA* provided the organization,

equipment, arms and training for the *Wehrmannschaft* until the beginning of 1942, when the German Order Police and SS took over most of the duties involved for what was now a full strength battalion. The ranks of the *Wehrmannschaft* men never changed however, and they kept referring to themselves using the *"SA"* prefix. For example, the commander of the initial *Wehrmannschaft* battalion formed was referred to as *SA-Sturmbannfuehrer* Toescher. In April, 1942 service in the *Wehrmannschaft* became mandatory for all ethnic Germans living in both newly created German provinces. At this time, German census figures showed that exactly 87,400 men were available for call-up in the *Untersteiermark* province, as well as 17,592 in the province of *Oberkrain*. It appears that the *Wehrmannschaft* battalion was now given the position as an auxiliary police formation and named *"Wehrmannschaftsbataillon Sued"* (Defense Militia Battalion "South") in April/May 1942.

This unit's ascension as an auxiliary to the SS, police, and *Gendarmerie* forces in the country was as a direct result of the increase in guerrilla activity. The *Wehrmannschaft* was gradually expanded over the course of 1942 into two, then three battalions, and by 1943 it was a reinforced regiment with five full strength battalions. At its height, it contained around 6,000+ men.

The remaining tens of thousands of potential *Wehrmannschaft* recruits were not called for service, mainly due to their need to tend to the crops, and to run other sectors of the local economy necessary for the war effort, but many served part-time as *"Selbstschutz"* (self defense) guards in static posts, mostly dependent on where they lived and worked. This began to take shape in 1942, and by May of the same year, there were seven such *Selbstschutz* platoons operating throughout the two provinces. These *Selbstschutz* platoons were made subordinate to the local *Gendarmerie* post where they were located.

A training company for the first *Wehrmannschaft* battalion was established in Maribor (Marburg), and eventually each battalion was assigned a training company. The fifth battalion to be formed, named *"Mitte"* ("Center") was simply a grouping together of these various training companies, but this did not occur until late 1943. When formed, this 5th (training) battalion was posted to Maribor.

Operations during 1942 by the *Wehrmannschaft* mainly dealt with augmenting the meager German SS, police, and *Gendarmerie* forces that existed in the two provinces. Patrols and small, brief skirmishes with the Slovenian guerrillas took up most of the year, but there was one major significantly large engagement in which the *Wehrmannschaft* was employed, alongside substantially strong German forces. This was launched in the *Oberkrain (Gorenjska)* region, where the Germans employed for the very first time, their newly formed 18th Police Mountain Regiment, complete with three police rifle battalions, and a police mountain artillery battalion- all of them trained in mountain warfare. This police regiment was actually earmarked for front-line service in northern Finland, but was to receive its baptism of fire against the Slovene partisans.

The drive was to last from June until July 27th, 1942. In attendance for this drive were several high ranking Nazi Party, SS, & Police officials and included *SS-Obergruppenfuehrer* Dr. Alois Friedrich Rainer, the *"Gauleiter"* (Nazi Party District Leader) for Carinthia, and head of the civilian administration for *Oberkrain* (Upper Krajina) and *Untersteiermark* (Lower Styria), *SS-Gruppenfuehrer und Generalleutnant der Waffen-SS und Polizei* Erwin Roesner, in command of the Higher-SS & Police Command *"ALPENLAND"* (XVIII.SS Military District), and *SS-Oberstgruppenfuehrer und Generaloberst der Polizei* Kurt Daluege, who was the head of the German *Ordnungspolizei* (Order Police).

Wehrmannschaftsbataillon "Sued" was used in company and platoon-sized units to assist each of the police mountain rifle battalions. They not only helped to guide the police units, but also served in such auxiliary roles as interpreters, scouts, and flank protection for the advancing German police units.

The subject of the attack was the encirclement of the Partisan 2nd Group of Detachments (regiment in size) and the 1st Battalion of the 1st Group of Detachments. Although the drive was to have lasted until July, it continued into August with the 18th Police Mountain Regiment, *Wehrmann-schaftsbataillon "Sued"*, and other smaller police, SS, and SD forces carrying the drive through the localities of Blegos, Pokljuka, Jelovca, the Steiner Alps, Tucheinartal. By September 5th, the Slovenian partisans had been pushed back to the Topolsica region, the 18th Regiment moved through that region bordering the Italian/German demarcation area in Slovenia. It was in the Topolsica area that the *Wehrmannschaft* reportedly burnt down the settlements of Smrekovec and Sv. Kriz in the first week of September. The reason given was that these small settlements had provided assistance to the withdrawing guerrillas.

The German command thought that the operation had gone so well that Dr. Alois Friedrich Rainer held a victory parade in Kranj (Krainburg) on September 27th, 1942 and announced that Oberkrain (Gorenjska) had been made "quiet" at last. It was a boast that would prove premature, for on October 23rd, 1942 the Partisan *"Pohorje"* Battalion attacked the German *Gendarmerie* post at Oplotnica, and destroyed it, also making sure to burn the local *Burgermeister's* building. In fact, this guerrilla battalion attacked over one hundred separate times during the last three months of 1942 before retiring for winter quarters at Trije zeblji na Pohurju where it would later be betrayed to the *Wehrmannschaft* and police during the winter of 1942-1943.

The next significant encounter between the *Wehrmannschaft* and the guerrillas was the destruction of the *"Pohorje"* Battalion during a battle during the night of January 7th-8th, 1943. This guerrilla battalion was given away by pro-German supporters during late December, 1942. The unit had been raiding local farms and towns for foodstuffs and other supplies needed to keep them operational during the hard winter, and it was one of these farmers, angered by the pilfering, who turned them in to the German authorities.

The operation was quickly prepared by the *Befehlshaber der Ordnungspolizei "Alpenland"* (Commander of the Order Police "Alpine Region") and numbered *"Einsatzbefehl Nr. 106"* (Operational Order Number 106), dated January 6th, 1943. The text of the command noted that a strong guerrilla unit of battalion strength had been identified in a region about 20 kilometers southwest of Maribor (Marburg), and that a small reconnaissance force, sent in as a pathfinder unit, had already detected at least 30 partisans encamped in this heavily forested area.

The attacking police units were to be split up into four sectors, which would advance into the cordoned area, blocking the withdrawal or destroying any partisans that they encountered along the way until all sector units converged, and the enemy was either killed or captured. The units and assigned for the operation and their sectors were as follows:

Sector I - *Hauptmann der Schutzpolizei* Plecko
4th Company/ Police Guard Battalion I Vienna
2nd Company/ Police Guard Battalion Wiesbaden
5th Company/ Police Guard Battalion Alpenland
staging area: Leppe

Sector II - *Hauptmann der Schutzpolizei* Kreipel
3rd Company/ Police Regiment 19
Reserve Rural Police Company (motorized) Alpenland 1
Rural Police Station Company Marburg (Maribor)
staging area: Osojnka

Sector III - *Hauptmann* Winkler
350 men of the *Wehrmacht*
staging area: NW of Jaworski Vrh

Sector IV - *SA-Sturmbannfuehrer* Toescher
Defense Militia Battalion
staging area: W of Leppe

Accompanying the *Wehrmannschaft* Battalion was Franz Steindl, the head of the *Heimatbund* in Stajerska (Styria). The German officer in overall charge of this anti-guerrilla operation was *SS-Standartenfuehrer* Otto Lurker, Chief of the Security Police & SD forces in Styria. The battle began at around 4:30 in the morning, with the German police forces approaching undiscovered. The majority of the guerrilla battalion was caught by surprise because most were sleeping in their wooden bunkers, partly buried into the ground. After the battle, dozens of bodies littered the snow covered forest.

By 1943 the Slovenian guerrilla menace had increased to such proportions that before the year was out, the *Wehrmannschaft* battalions would number five and be stationed in the following localities:

"Mitte" (reserve)	Maribor (Marburg)
"Nord"	Bled
"West"	Kranj (Krainburg)
"Sued"	Celje (Cilli)
"Ost"	Maribor (Marburg)

It was in 1943 that the Wehrmannschaft battalions were numbered consecutively from I-V as follows:

"Sued"	Ist
"West"	IInd
"Nord"	IIIrd
"Ost"	IVth
"Mitte"	Vth

Support for these auxiliary police battalions came in the way of additional police units being sent to the region. In late February or early March, 1944 the reinforced 13th SS Police Regiment made its appearance in the Upper Carinthia (Oberkrain) region. The 14th SS Police Regiment, which had been operating out of Ogulin, Croatia since September, 1943, was shifted to Upper Carinthia in February, 1944. The 28th SS Police Regiment "Todt" was similarly sent to the Oberkrain region in the same month. In August, 1944 the Ist Battalion of SS Police Regiment 25 was transferred to Celje (Cilli).

In January, 1945 the Ist Battalion/ SS Police Regiment "Alpenvorland" was transferred to Upper Carinthia. SS Police Regiment 17 &

"Nagel" were also transferred to this region in late 1944. In October, 1944 the *Wehrmannschaftsregiment Untersteiermark*, along with the thousands of Selbstschutz were incorporated into the German *Volkssturm*. They performed garrison and anti-partisan duty and followed the German withdrawal into Austria in late April, 1945.

Slovenski Narodni Varnostni Zbor (Slovene National Security Force)

On November 12th, 1943 a Slovenian Home Guard Lieutenant-Colonel by the name of Anton (Tone) Kokalj, originating from the western Slovenian province of Primorska, raised a new Slovene collaborationist force called the SNVZ, or *Slovenski Narodni Varnostni Zbor* (the Slovene National Security Force) in the port of Koper. Colonel Kokalj had received permission to raise this force not only from SS General Erwin Roesner, but SS General Odilo Globocnik, who was head of the Higher-SS & Police Command "Adriatic Coast". This latter SS command was responsible for the three northeastern regions of Italy bordering Austria and Slovenia. This area and the Primorska region of Slovenia would be the area where the SNVZ would be employed.

Initially and during its entire life span, recruiting efforts for the unit would be hampered by two problems. The first was the fact that the Italian Army had drafted Slovenians into its forces in Africa during their reign over the region. Many of these Slovenians had been either captured or had surrendered to the British Commonwealth forces there. Later many were recruited for the Royal Yugoslav Army in exile which was being organized in Yugoslavia. The second problem lay in the fact that by late 1943 the war was clearly

turning against the Axis, so recruits were not so forthcoming.

The headquarters for the SNVZ was set up in Triest, and soon Colonel Kokalj had several companies of volunteers. Colonel Franc Krenner was able to supply Colonel Kokalj with some Domobranci officers which would help train the new recruits. In March, 1944 an SNVZ Urban Police force was established in the major cities and towns:

SNVZ Police Unit	Location
Triest Company	Triest (Trst)
Gorizia Company	Gorizia (Gorica)
1st Platoon	Pula
2nd Platoon	Koper
3rd Platoon	Rijeka
4th Platoon	Idrija
5th Platoon	Postojna

An SNVZ Rural Police force ("Orozniski Zbor") was also established almost a year later (in February, 1945) but this force never got past the preliminary stages. The numbers of volunteers continued to come in drips and drops, but by August, 1944 the organization reached its peak strength of 1,782 men in sixteen rifle companies. These companies were spread out into four regions as follows:

Postojna:	Triest Province
Gorica:	Gorica Province
Ilirska Bistrica:	Rijeka Province
Idrija:	Rijeka Province

Initially, these SNVZ rifle companies were spread out amongst the vast countryside, and as a result, were only able to offer no offensive capabilities and minimal defensive ability. In order to change this and to make the SNVZ a more effective, anti-partisan force, SS General Odilo Globocnik decreed on October 27th, 1944 that the SNVZ companies were to concentrate in the region between Postojna and Ilirska Bistrica, where they would be regrouped into four battalions (numbered 1-4) which would be controlled by a newly raised SNVZ regimental headquarters. The designation of the regiment was "1st Slovenian Coastal Assault Regiment."

Each SNVZ battalion contained four rifle companies and one heavy weapons company. In December, 1944 this SNVZ regiment was moved to an area between Postojna and Idrija and assigned railroad security duty and other traffic communication. Their main enemy was the Slovenian Partisan 9th Corps. The SNVZ Regiment employed three of its four battalions, since the 2nd Battalion was designated as the training unit for the regiment and remained located in the town of Postojna. In February, 1945 this 2nd Battalion was redesignated as the *"Reservna dezelna bramba"* (Reserve Defense Force). Its commander at this time was Major Sinkovec, a Domobranci officer who had been assigned to the SNVZ directly from Ljubljana.

By the fall of 1944 the Slovene 9th Partisan Corps had established a stronghold northeast of Gorizia, and had disrupted rail and road traffic so completely that SS General Odilo Globocnic was forced to launch a major anti-guerrilla operation. This was begun on December 19th, 1944 and would last until the end of the month. Its objective was nothing less than the destruction of the 9th Partisan Corps. A total of around 5,000 men were used. The units employed included a variety of formations:

- 1st Regiment, Serbian Volunteer Corps, located in Postojna with 500 men.
- 10th SS Police Regiment, with 1,200 men in three battalions
- Police Volunteer Battalion "Gorizia" (Italians under German Order Police), 323 men.
- 2nd (Italian) Fusilier Battalion, with 260 men
- 1st Slovenian Coastal Assault Regiment, 1,500 men split into four battalions.
- 14th (Italian) Frontier Battalion, with 522 men.
- 4th (Italian) National Republican Guard Regiment, with 750 men.
Total Strength: 5,055 men.

As was usual, the number of troops was not sufficient to keep the guerrillas from slipping through some openings in the lines, and most of the force was able to escape.[11] In February, 1945 the command & control of the SNVZ regiment was disrupted, when Colonel Anton (Tone) Kokalj was killed in action. While a replacement was sought, SS Major Georg Michalsen assumed command of the regiment, until April when Major Janko Dabeljak assumed control.

The next major operation in which the SNVZ regiment took part in was another anti-partisan drive begun in early March, 1945 and code-named "Ruebezahl." This time, the Axis forces were trying to destroy the partisan forces in the town of Lokve. This attack was launched by two separate combat groups. The first group (3,000 strong) was code-named "Zuschneid" and was made up of three SS Police battalions from the 10th SS Police Regiment and the 1st Slovenian Coastal Assault Regiment. The second combat group, comprising 2,500 men and code-named "Koestermann," was made up of two battalions of the 730th Infantry Regiment (710th Infantry Division), plus a small German/Italian police company and a platoon of engineers.

Operation "Ruebezahl" was deemed moderately successful, and the town of Lokve and its surroundings was temporarily cleared of guerrillas. A third and final offensive was launched by the SNVZ regiment and other forces under the command of the Higher-SS & Police Leader "Adriatic Coast" on March 19th, 1945. This operation lasted until April 7th but was an overall disappointment, since the 9th Partisan Corps was able to once again escape the trap. The Regiment remained in the Gorizia area until it surrendered to the British 8th Army in May, 1945.

[11]Petelin, Stanko. "Osvoboditev Slovenskega Primorja." Nova Gorica, 1966, pages 80-83.

Photographic Section

Above: SS-Obergruppenfuehrer Dr. Alois Friedrich Rainer, the "Gauleiter" (District Leader) for Carinthia, and head of the Nazi civilian administration in Upper Kraina ("Oberkrain"), and in Lower Styria ("Untersteiermark"). These areas were annexed from Slovenia to Germany when Yugoslavia was defeated by the Axis in 1941. After the war, Rainer was caught in Austria and extradicted to Yugoslavia. He was tried in Ljubljana and hanged in 1946.

At right, SS General Roesner is seen congratulating some Slovene Home Guardsmen. Colonel Franc Krenner (back turned to the camera) is also present. Notice the German Order Police officer on the extreme right hand side of the picture. The German police presence in training, arming, and directing the Domobrans was extensive.

Below left: SS Major General & Lt. General of the Police Odilo Globocnik. Globocnik's task was to combat the growing guerrilla menace of the Italian & Slovenian partisans in the regions of northeast Italy and the Istrian peninsula. On June 6th, 1945 (almost one month after the end of the war) he was caught in the Kara-wankan Alps of southern Austria by a British patrol. Rather than be put on trial and almost certainly be hanged, he opted to take his own life by biting on a poisoned vial hidden in his teeth. Reich-fuehrer SS Heinrich Himmler killed himself in this same manner and under similar circumstances.

Above right: A very rare photo of Leon Rupnik in the uniform of Inspector General of the Home Guard, alongside Bishop Roznan & SS General Roesner, sometime in 1945.

Right: Another rare photo of General Leon Rupnik, this time with his son, Vuk Rupnik, who was a Colonel in the Slovenian Home Guard.

Right: SS General Odilo Globocnik gives the Nazi salute in Triest, some time in 1944. The NSDAP (Nazi Party) leader whose view is obstructed by Globocnik's right arm is none other than Oberbereichs-leiter Pfeiffer, the NSDAP leader in charge of Triest and its surrounding areas. An NSDAP Hauptbereichs-leiter can be seen behind Globocnik and Pfeiffer. Notice the presence of Italian GNR troops in the background.

Center Right: The SS officer in the center (wearing glasses) is SS Sturmbannfuehrer (SS Major) Ernst Lerch, who was Odilo Globocnik's Chief-of-Staff. The other SS officer (on Lerch's left side), is SS Haupt-sturmfuehrer (SS Captain) Schindlmayr, also on Globocnik's staff. The Chetnik officer with them (extreme left) is Momcilo Djujic, leader of the Serbian Chetnik "Dinara" Brigade.

Below Right: Wearing the soft cover is Bundesfuehrer, SA-Oberfuehrer Franz Steindl, leader of the ethnic German Wehrmannschaft Regiment, on the occasion of Hitler Youth leader Arthur Axmann's visit to Marburg (Maribor) in 1944.

Below Left: Dr. Siegfried Uberreither, the Chief of the Nazi Civilian Administration in Stajerska, also known as "Untersteier-mark" (Lower Styria) in German.

Above: parade of the Wehrmann-schaft in Marburg (Maribor) some *time in 1944. The parade was organized in honor of Reichs-* *jugendfuehrer Arthur Axmann. Axmann can be seen giving the Nazi salute in the bottom right photo in the previous page. Dr. Siegfried Uberreither is seen in that same photograph, immediately behind Axmann.*

Center left: Inspector General of the Domobranci (Home Guard) Leon Rupnik, seen here shaking hands with various German officers. The German officer at the extreme right is probably the commander of the 54th Organization Todt (construction) Battalion, since the cloth emblem on his left overcoat sleeve bears that unit's designation. The 54th was not a locally raised unit, neither was it formed in nearby Austria. It was organized in Pommerania.

Left: some more NSDAP (Nazi Party) officials from the region. In the center of the photograph we again see a Wehrmannschaft commander, this one an unknown SS Standartenfuehrer.

Right: Wehrmannschaft Day, sometime in 1944. Here we see SS General Erwin Roesner, smiling (extreme right), together with what initially appears to be a junior ranking Gebirgsjaeger (German army mountain) officer. A close examination reveals that this Army officer is none other than General Eduard Dietl, the "hero" of Narvik. He eventually led the German 20th Mountain Army in northern Finland. On his return trip from his tour of Slovenia, he was killed when his plane crashed into the Austrian alps. Roesner's entourage includes Nazi Party, SS, Army, Organization Todt, and other officials belonging to his XVIIIth SS Military District Headquarters "Alpenland". This photo was taken near the village of Spodnja Vizinga (about 23 kilometers west of Marburg (Maribor).

Center right: Colonel Franc Krenner (back to photo) with staff members of the 18th SS Military District. A close examination of the cuff band on the officer in the right of the photo shows it to read: " ALPENLAND".

Center left: SD Untersturmfuehrer Druschke, from the town of Jesenice in the "Oberkrain" region of Slovenia. The Yugoslav government tried unsuccessfully to extradict Druschke after the war was over.

Bottom right: Leon Rupnik (left of photo), an unknown Ordnungs-polizei officer, and (extreme right), NSDAP (Nazi Party) Oberbefehlsleiter Hilgenfeldt.

BIN DER BANDIT "UBO"
HEISSE **KARL KOS** UND STAME-KISOWETZ
BIN SEIT 15.4.42. BEI DEN BANDEN UND
HABE AM ÜBERFALL AUF DEN GENDAR=
MERIEPOSTEN MORAUTSCH IN OBERKRAIN
ERMORDUNG V. 2 GENDARMEN, PLÜNDERUNG
EINES KAUFHAUSES IN MORAUTSCH,
ERMORDUNG D. AUFSICHTSJÄGERS
GORISCHEK U. UEBERFALL AUF

Top Left: In the beginning, captured guerrillas were labelled as bandits, like Slovenian national hero Karl Kos, who was charged with killing two Gendarmes and plundering the post. The sign reads: "I am the bandit 'Ubo.' On April 15th, 1942 Karl Kos and a cadre surprised the Gendarmerie post in Morautsch, Oberkrain...."

Top Right: Summary execution for Franc Sesek, from Bukovina. He was shot near Smlednik, between Kranj and Ljubljana on August 22nd, 1941

Center Left: German police officers walking around the remains of eight Slovenian civilians (some of them women), who were shot near Krajinskaya on August 5th, 1941. They had been accused of being members of the Partisan Kranj Battalion (or of supporting the guerrillas).

Above: The Order Police emblem.

Below Left: December 12th, 1941. The German police recover the dead bodies of twelve German Gendarmes killed when their 46 man platoon was ambushed by Slovenian partisans.

The main occupation force which the Germans employed in occupied Slovenia during the period between May 1941 and the spring of 1942 were the small and dispersed Gendarmerie, SD and Order Police posts located throughout the two main provinces of Oberkrain and Untersteiermark.

Extreme right: German Order Police and (in the background) SD officers conferring before an anti-guerilla drive in the Gorenjska ("Oberkrain") region of Slovenia, July 1942. The Germans & Italians began to launch major anti-partisan offensives in Slovenia beginning in that year.

Below center: German Soldiers place their dead on a truck for transport to a proper burial site, June 1942. Twenty-seven Germans were killed by Slovenian guerrillas of the 1st Detachment/ 2nd Battalion. No prisoners were taken by either side. If captured, both sides would eventually shoot the prisoner(s). This guerrilla war was a cruel one, with no quarter asked nor given.

Below right: July 1st, 1942. The partisans had just blown up a bridge vital to the Germans in the Oberkrain region. In reprisal, thirty local inhabitants were rounded up and shot. One managed to crawl away and report the incident. Here the dead lie beside a stone wall.

Below: A captured partisan (2nd from left) caught near Blegos between 3-5 August, 1942.

Above: Cloth emblem of the SS & Police forces.

Alpenland

Above: Cuff band worn on the lower left sleeve of the tunic. This was worn by staff members of the XVIIIth SS Military District

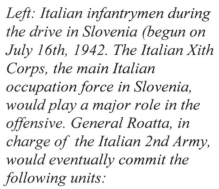

Left: Italian infantrymen during the drive in Slovenia (begun on July 16th, 1942. The Italian Xith Corps, the main Italian occupation force in Slovenia, would play a major role in the offensive. General Roatta, in charge of the Italian 2nd Army, would eventually commit the following units:
105th Black Shirt Legion
22nd Cacciatori di Alpi Division
Prince Eugene of Savoy Cavalry
14th Isonzo & 153rd Macerata Divisions 11th Bersaglieri Regiment the 57th Lombardia Division, plus Slovenian White Guard units, including the newly created "Legion of Death".

Below left & right: Italian flame thrower armored car & mortar crew.

Left: Column of Italian infantry during the 1942 summer offensive against the Slovene partisans. This photo was taken in the Dolenjska region.

Left: Dead guerrillas from the IIIrd Battalion of the Lankar Brigade. This guerrilla brigade unsuccessfully attacked the town of Kocevje (in the Dolenjska region) on March 16th, 1943. the Italian and White Guard units were able to repel them..

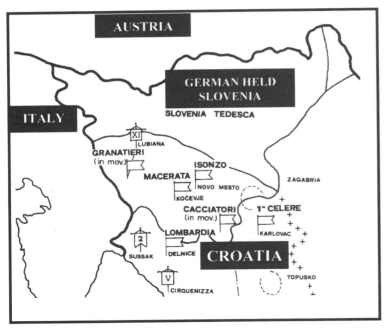

Above: Location of the major Italian divisions under Xith Corps in Slovenia, September 1942.

Above Right: Two captured Slovenian guerrillas are blindfolded before being executed by Italian Alpini troops, summer of 1942.

Right: Execution by firing squad of a Slovenian partisan, fall of 1942. While the Germans were more severe in their anti-guerilla methods, the Italian military did not hesitate to employ similar methods.

Right: An Italian member of the Black Shirt (Fascist) militia and some Slovenian village militiamen. The Italians supplied NCO's (usually CCNN troops, as in this case) in order to arm and train their collaborationist forces. The Village Guard were static, self-defense troops made up of farmers stationed in their local village or hamlet.

Left: In the beginning, the White Guard did not possess a specific uniform, so all types of military and civilian clothing was worn.. Black berets were common. When the Slovenian White Guard were merged into the Italian "Milizia Voluntare Anti Comunista" they began to receive insignia and some semblance of a uniform. In 1942 the Black berets appeared. The Village Guard favored these berets but they were also worn by the Legion of Death. A metallic sword and shield emblem was worn pinned on the front of the beret.

Center left: Notice the sword and shield emblem on the beret of the volunteer on the extreme right of this photo. Notice also the skull and crossed bones metallic pin back on the cover of the man sitting in the center of the photo. The Legion of Death wore this emblem, although enough photographic evidence exists to show that both emblems were worn indiscriminately by both local defense (Village Guard) and anti-guerilla (Legion of Death) forces.

Bottom left & right: two examples of White Guard commanders- Remskar (from Log near Ljubljana) and Franc Kremsar with Father Peter Kriraj of the Catholic League.

Above left: Another example of the ad-hoc uniforms worn in the early days of the White Guard. Notice that he is wearing the Skull & Crossed Bones metallic pin-back insignia over his left breast pocket.

Right above, center, and bottom: Mokronog, Dolenjska - September 1942. The 1,600 strong Legion of Death parades just before being committed to battle. General Robotti inspected this newly raised anti-Communist formation on September 10th, 1942. The Legion of Death was partly clad in former Yugoslav Army uniform, but as these photos show, they also had a sprinkling of civilian atire. The helmet types included Yugoslav, Cezch, and even many of French manufacture.

In the spring of 1942 the Italians delivered about 2,500 used tropical light brown uniforms (originally manufactured for use by Italian forces in North & East Africa) and gave them to the Slovenian White Guard.

picture was taken no later than the springtime of 1942 (when these uniforms were supplied).

Top left: Another view of the Legion of Death formation. The Slovenian Communist guerillas have admitted that it was the Legion of Death which gave them the most trouble, since it was a unit composed local inhabitants, thoroughly knowledgable in the terrain and her people; And mainly made up of Catholic Youth members who were rabidly anti-Communist. The Legion of Death was such a highly effective and motivated combat unit that it was never defeated in battle by the Partisans.
s

Left center: Slovene MVAC commander Franc Korenc. Notice that on the side of the beret is the MVAC rank insignia (a cloth or metallic five-pointed star on a colored cloth triangle) The color of the triangular cloth and star denoted the rank of the individual wearing this device. Korenc appears to be wearing the light brown Italian tropical uniform underneath his trenchcoat, indicating that this

Below left: Dolenjska region, early 1943. The Italians inspect an honor guard made up of Italian troops and White Guard militiamen. Notice that by 1943 the White Guard had a definite uniform. All are wearing white shirts, berets (complete with the metallic sword and shield emblem), black blouses and trousers, complete with matching black overcoats. In the case of the White Guard officer, he has been provided with black high boots.

1943-

Right: A perfect example of the new Italian tropical uniforms that were distributed to the White Guard in 1942.

Center right: A White Guard unit from the Dobrova post at Gaberje moves out against the Dolomiti Partisan Detachment, March 15th through the 21st, 1943.

Center below: Captured Partisans are shot execution style by the White Guard.

Right: The Slovenian poet and guerilla, Ivan Rob (2nd from the right) is led to his death by Italian soldiers and White Guard troops. Ivan Rob was not only a poet, but was head of propaganda for the Partisan Lankar Brigade. He was captured on January 21st, 1943. A month later (in February) he was shot at Ligojna, near Vrhnika.

Bottom Right: Insignia of the Legion of Death Regiment. These two Death's Head emblems were produced by the Italians and used by the Legion of Death. The were made of tin and were metallic in appearance. They were pinned back on the beret or over the left breast of the tunic.

Left: Turjak Castle under attack by the Partisan "Presen" Brigade. Recently armed and equipped with captured Italian heavy weapons (including tanks and artillery pieces), they surrounded the 1,600 man White & Blue Guard forces in and around Turjak Castle and eventually forced their surrender.

Center left: September 19th, 1943 - captured nationalist forces are lined up. The partisans had promised that no White or Blue Guard leaders would be killed if the nationalists would only surrender, but that promise was not kept.

Left and right: Turjak Castle after the battle. The scars of the siege are clearly visible.

Top right: Turjak Castle and the town of Turjak after it was recaptured from the Partisans in October, 1943. The Germans used the bulk of the 19th SS Police Regiment, augmented by newly regrouped Home Guard forces to recapture this area (located about 20 kilometers south-southeast of Ljubljana).

Center right: As December, 1943 rolled around, the town of Turjak remained in Axis control. Here we see two Home Guard soldiers walking on a snow covered road in Turjak.

Center left: Slovene Home Guard soldier. When the Germans assumed control of the remnants of the White Guard in late 1943, they set out to reorganize and newly outfit the Slovene nationalist forces. In the beginning, Italian insignia was still worn, as shown by the use of a Legion of Death emblem by this trooper.

Bottom right: Slovenian Domobranci (Home Guard) during the fall of 1943. The diverse uniforms can still be seen. The dependence on Italian weapons is still clearly visible. As time wore on, the Germans would supply more and more German weapons, clothing, and unique insignia.

Left: A Slovene Home Guard squad wearing the early pattern uniforms. The machine-gunner in the center of the photo is wearing the initial (triangular) cap cockade bearing the Slovene national colors of white-blue-red.

Left Center: The same squad holding six machine guns which appear to be the 7.92mm M37 (Yugoslav) SMG, and the Italian Breda model 30 6.4mm SMG (extreme right hand of the photo).

Below: Another early photograph showing the use of Italian and Yugoslav uniforms and equipment. Note the "Village Guard" emblem worn on the right sleeve of the soldier kneeling on the extreme left of the photo. Three Italian Breda model 30 SMG's

Left: three brothers. The one on the right is still wearing what appears to be the earlier uniform, including the Yugoslav soft cover.

are also seen. The early pattern triangular cockade is also clearly seen on their Yugoslav soft covers.

Right: December 18th, 1943. The Slovene Home Guard held a funeral mass and military procession in Ljubljana for Home Guardsmen killed fighting the Partisan 14th Division. In the background on the hill is Ljubljana Castle, the location of the Slovene HQ staff.

Below Center: Platoon upon platoon of Home Guard troops line up for the parade which would enter the city for the funeral mass at the city center (see above right). The parade would then continue up to Ljubljana Castle, where the dead soldiers would be buried.

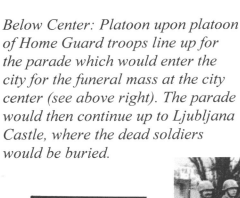

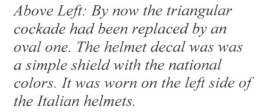

Above Left: By now the triangular cockade had been replaced by an oval one. The helmet decal was was a simple shield with the national colors. It was worn on the left side of the Italian helmets.

Above Right: With the Church in the background, the Slovene Home Guard parade crosses the famous "three-bridges" located in the city center. An officer on horseback leads this particular Home Guard column.

Left: The parade continued through the streets of Ljubljana. The Slovene shield, which included the national eagle in blue on a white background can be seen on the left sleeve of the Home Guard overcoats.

Above Center: The gun carriages which were used to carry the dead Home Guard soldiers.

Left: The parade winds its way up to Ljubljana Castle for the burial.

49

1944-

Below: A Slovene Home Guard post, somewhere in the countryside. The Yugoslav 7.92mm M37 SMG is once again seen here. This submachine-gun could fire at the rate of 500-550 rounds per minute. Snow is seen on the ground.

Right: General Leon Rupnik pays his last respects to the fallen Slovene Home Guard soldiers. Behind him is Colonel Franc Krenner. Other high ranking Home Guard officers who attended this funeral included Lieutenant-Colonel Polhov Gradec, and the

Above Left: The left shoulder board as worn by General Rupnik. It was composed of a gold background with silver braids and a brass button. This insignia was worn on both shoulders. The officers from major to colonel also had a gold backing with a silver piping and silver stars. Warrant officers to captains had a silver background with gold stars, while enlisted and NCO's had a dark green background with silver or gold bars (depending on rank).

bespectacled Colonel Vizjak.

Right: Two Slovene Home Guardsmen during the winter of 1943-44. The trooper on the left is holding an Italian "Barti" automatic gun. The one on the right has a British "sten" gun.

Left: Slovenian Home Guard troops and German SS police troops line up and count the dead guerrillas killed in an ambush. This battle took place on March 16th, 1944 near the town of Javorica.
The Partisan unit which fell into the Axis trap was the 4th Battalion of the "Lankar" Brigade. The whole countryside is still covered with snow. The winter months were typically the hardest for the guerrillas, since it was difficult to obtain rations and to move.

Left Center: Another photo showing the carnage of the battle. Here we also see dead horses, used by the partisans to haul their heavy weapons and equipment. A Slovenian Home Guard officer can be seen in the bvackground, left hand pointing in the distance, while the soldiers seem to be searching the bodies for any type of documents.

Bottom Left: The Slovenian Home Guard forces also took losses. Here we see four Home Guardsmen carrying a stretcher on which they've laid a wounded comrade. The trooper on the right side is wearing an Italian camouflage smock, very popular among the Slovene Domobranci.

Above right: The original triangular cockade worn on the solft covers.

The triangular cockade was in use as late as the middle of 1944, but by the end of the year, the oval cockade had replaced it. A later version of the Oval cockade included the Slovenian national eagle.

Below Left: Two German officers examine the carcasses of two horses,   *Right: The late-model cockade being worn.*

killed during the fire-fight that killed around 60+ members of the Partisan 4th Battalion / Lankar Brigade.

Center Right: An extremely rare photograph of a Slovene artillery battery. The piece is of Italian manufacture. There were only three artillery batteries that were formed by the Home Guard. This one, located in Velike Lasce, was the 3rd Battery.

Right: An artillery piece belonging to the 1st Battery, located in Ljubljana. The 2nd Battery was also stationed in that city. The two officers on the extreme right of the picture are none other than Colonel Vuk Rupnik & Colonel Tone Kokalj.

Top Left: Ljubljana Stadium, April 20th, 1944. Here we see recently trained Slovenian Home Guard recruits, undergoing the swearing in ceremony, on the occasion of Adolf Hitler's 55th birthday. Notice the presence of German Order Police officials. The German SS & Police command was instrumental in raising, organizing, and directing the Slovenian Domobranci.
In 1944, the German High Command announced that that Slovene troops, recruited from the Stajerska region of the country, had won 50 Iron Crosses, 1st Class while more than one thousand had received the Iron Cross, 2nd Class.

Left Center: The top German and Slovene leadership in the area inspect the new recruits. Leon Rupnik, with his very conspicuous white beard, can be clearly seen, this time wearing civilian clothes. SS General Erwin Roesner is seen giving the Nazi salute, while Colonel Franc Krenner is seen walking behind and to the left of Roesner and Order Police Colonel Rossbacker. In the background is an Italian tank.

Left: A closer photo of the officers. In the background is a Slovenian policeman. He wears the peaked cap and Slovene shield on his left arm. Police officers were also sworn in on this day.

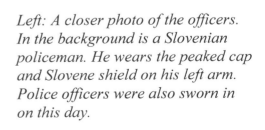

Top Right: Wounded Home Guard veterans receive the German Iron Cross, for bravery under fire. The wound badge was also awarded to any Domobran wounded in battle. Many ethnic German Slovenes served in the Wehrmacht. One, Warrant Officer Primozic, even made the front cover of the German propaganda magazine, "Signal."

Below Center: A wide angle view of Ljubljana Stadium and the forces arrayed for the ceremony. Two Italian assault guns can be clearly

seen. The Slovenian flag, presented in length, is shown. The Slovenian national colors were white-blue-red (in that order). The Domobranci insignia represented this color scheme.

Right: Parade of the Home Guard through the streets of Ljubljana on the same day (20th April, 1944).

Top Left: April 23rd, 1944. Colonel Franc Krenner (2nd from left), seen here shaking hands with an unknown officer. The helmet is Czech made, and has been painted in a camouflage pattern. By the spring of 1944, this type of helmet had been mostly replaced with the Italian or German helmet. The uniform of the officer also seems to be ex-Yugoslav in origin.

Below Right: A very interesting

Above Left: A perfect example of the triangular cockade, and early style mixture of Yugoslav/Italian uniforms (center), compared to the later version (German inspired & supplied) oval cockade & uniform.

photograph of a Home Guard trooper, wearing a German camouflage soft cover and the metallic mountain trooper insignia on the side of it.

Left: A Home Guard expedition winds its way through a Slovenian town, sometime in 1944. Notice the German covers and camouflage blouse.

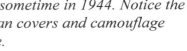

Far Right: Three brothers serving in the Home Guard. The man in the center is a staff sergeant, while his brothers flanking him are corporals.

Right: A Home Guard officer and his platoon leaders.

Center Left: SS General Erwin Roesner is decorating what initially appears to be German Order Police soldiers with the Iron Cross. A closer

examination of the soldier's shoulder boards indicate that they are Slovenian. The soldier on the extreme right is a corporal.

Center Right: Photograph of a Domobranci sergeant.

Right: Sergeant's soulder board..

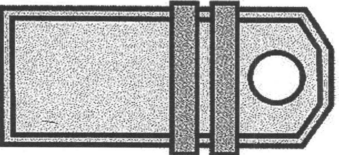

Above Left: The German Consular Office building in Ljubljana. Notice the German and Slovenian flags. What at first appears to be SS Police troops marching past the building is in reality a group of Slovenian volunteers serving in the Order Police. Most of the officers were Germans of the Order Police.

Left: Office of the German Police command in Ljubljana. The office is being guarded by Home Guard troopers. The Slovenian Home Guard battle flag can be seen. It apparently included the Slovenian national eagle (in blue) on a white shield, superimposed over the flag..

Top Right: Leon Rupnik, guarded by two Home Guardsmen, discusses a point with a local citizen.

Above Center Right: A group of Home Guardsmen take a rest during a patrol. The Home Guard officer in charge of the group has his back to the camera. By late 1944 Home Guard uniforms resembled more and more their German allies. The use of the Italian helmets and former Dutch uniforms (brought in large quantities by the Germans) were still in use, but German helmets and equipment came into more use.

Right: SSGeneral Erwin Roesner (center), accompanied by Colonel Franc Krenner (extreme left) visits a Home Guard unit during an inspection tour. Notice the German Order Police officer behind Roesner. He is wearing a camouflage cover. Behind the officer, in the foreground is a one man carriage next to a horse cart. Mobility for the Home Guard by late 1944 was a problem, due mainly to the decreased output of oil by Germany, and the consumption demands of the German armies in the main battlefronts.

Below: The cover of the September 28th, 1944 issue of "Slovensko Domobranstvo", the magazine of the Slovenian Home Guard. The magazine was published mainly to boost the morale of the Domobranci.

Above Left: December, 1944. General Leon Rupnik once again dons the uniform of Inspector General of the Domobranci. This time he is seen conferring with his son, Vuk Rupnik, who by then had been promoted to the rank of Colonel in the Home Guard. The end of 1944 brought more battles on the beleaguered German and Slovenian forces in that country. The Slovenian Partisan movement was now about 25,000 men strong, and was well organized into several partisan divisions. As time would tell, the coming year would bring more disasters to the Domobranci.

Left: November 12th, 1943- The Slovenian port of Koper, on the Adriatic coast, located on the northwest corner of the Istrian peninsula. Here we see recruits being placed on board numerous lorries of Italian origin. These volunteers were destined to join the SNVZ (Slovenski Narodni Varnostni Zbor), or Slovene National Security Force. Another term used was SVZ, or Slovenska varnostna straza (Slovenian Security Guard). Recruiting efforts seemed to have proved quite difficult, given that many Slovenes from this region of the country had already been conscripted into the Italian Army and most had been captured in North Africa, where many were recruited for the Royal Yugoslav Army, then forming in Egypt. Desertions also seemed to be a problem.

Below Left: Lieutenant-Colonel (later promoted to full colonel) Anton (Tone) Kokalj, who originated the idea to form the SNVZ. He is seen here wearing an Italian camouflage uniform. In fact, camouflage gear was quite popular among the SNVZ. The Headquarters of the SNVZ was located in Triest. Eventual strength would lead to just under 2,000 men in the entire formation.

A close examination of the left breast pocket reveals a badge worn by Anton Kokalj. It was a metallic, triangular shaped item showing (from top to bottom) the blue sky, below which are three white mountain peaks, and below that, a sun with its rays protruding upwards in all directions. This was probably a locally made award since rank insignia was usually worn on the shoulders, and was the standard Home Guard insignia. The soft cover cockade here seems to be the oval white, red, blue version, although one source states that the German police soft cover and its cockade was used without the German national eagle. The soft cover here seems to be ex-Dutch army.

According one Slovenian and one Italian reference, the SNVZ was directly under the control of SS General Odilo Globocnik, who was head of the "Higher-SS & Police Leader, Adriatic Coast." Both sources mention that between 1944-1945, the SNVZ was composed of four battalions. The actual date when the SNVZ companies were merged into battalions was October 24th, 1944. It was also at this time that a regimental headquarters was also raised in order to control these units. It was thus that the 1st Slovene Coastal Assault Regiment came into being.

Right: Colonel Kokalj (extreme right) with two other SNVZ officers. The German Order Police in Triest was instrumental in helping to raise and support Colonel Kokalj's SNVZ. In August, 1944 the strength of the SNVZ reached exactly 1,782 men. Eventually, sixteen rifle companies were organized. These companies were parceled out to individual towns and villages.

Below and Center Right: An SNVZ light mortar crew. The mortar is the Italian trench mortar. The SNVZ insignia (an red Illirian ship, blue sea, and white background) can be seen.

Below Right: A group of SNVZ men.. Although they wore some German uniforms, ex-Italian gear prevailed in the unit. The Italian jackets were primarily the opened style, for use with ties.

Left: Triest and the surrounding region. Part of the area of operations of the SNVZ.

KEY-
TRST: Triest
Gorica: Goricia
The Istrian Peninsula was located south of Triest.

Top Left: An SNVZ 2nd Lieutenant instructs two recruits on the Italian 40mm trench mortar. The soft covers and uniforms of the recruits appear to be German made, while the officer seems to be wearing the ex-Dutch army uniform that was supplied to the Home Guard in large quantaties by the Germans. The sixteen rifle companies were split up into four regions which the SNVZ was charged with guarding:

Postojna:	Triest Province
Gorica:	Gorica Province
Ilirska Bistrica:	Rijeka Province
Idria:	Rijeka Province

Center & Bottom Left: An excellent view of the Italian style open blouse. This style of uniform was also used by the men of the SNVZ, and black ties were common. However, in a throwback to earlier times, many of the 16 rifle companies tended to wear one distinctly colored tie in lieu of the black tie. This was done to differentiate one company from another.

In the case of the center left photograph, this 2nd Lieutenant appears to be wearing a German camouflage blouse. The mixture of Italian & German uniforms was quite common, and generally, there was less order in the SNVZ than in the regular Home Guard units when it came to uniformity of the uniforms.

Notice in the bottom left photo that two out of the five soldiers pictured happen to be quite young- another hint at the difficulty that this unit encountered when they attempted to recruit from the local Slovenian population.

Bottom Photo: A perfect example of the variety of uniforms used. Notice the SNVZ shield on the man in the right of the photo.

Below Left: An SNVZ member with the Italian Breda 6.5mm model 30 SMG .

Below Right: An SNVZ 2nd Lt. instructs a soldier in the use of the Italian Breda model 30 submachine gun.

Left: Vuk Rupnik, the son of Leon Rupnik is seen here (center, pointing). This photograph was taken just outside of Ljubljana Castle, which stood on a hill in the center of the city. While Vuk Rupnik wears the Home Guard emblem, the officer carrying the briefcase (behind Rupnik) seems to be wearing the SNVZ emblem. This officer is non other than Colonel Tone Kokalj.

Bottom Left: A group of SNVZ soldiers line up for lunch. The meal seems to be either a soup or stew.

Slovenian partisan strength continued to grow steadily from September, 1943 onwards. Altogether during the war, 41 partisan "brigades" were formed. Five were organized in 1942 (of which one was disbanded); Twenty-three were formed in 1943 (of which 10 were disbanded); Nine were raised in 1944 (of which one was disbanded); And four more were formed in 1945, two which established outside of Slovenia, and four entirely manned by Italian guerrillas. This is contrast to the small, 2,500 man Slovenian partisan force in 1941.

Below: A captured Italian L6 tank put to use by the Slovenian partisans.

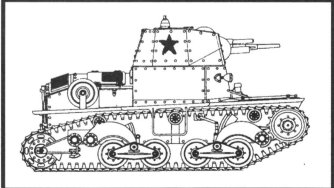

1945-

Top Right: Ljubljana, February, 1945. With the Partisans quickly gaining the upper hand in the countryside, Leon Rupnik, prepared to fight till the end, dons the uniform of General of the Domobranci.

Center Right: January, 1945. Colonel Vuk Rupnik, Leon Rupnik's son, is shown here (extreme left) receiving the Iron Cross for gallantry in the face of the enemy. Notice the Iron Cross pinned to his 2nd coat button. Other officers of the Home Guard appear in this photograph.

Bottom Right: Not Germans, but Slovenian volunteers serving in the Home Guard. By 1945, the use of German uniforms and equipment became more common, but the ex-Dutch Army uniforms were not completely done away with.

The year 1945 was to prove the final undoing of the Axis forces in Europe and Asia. With military reverses on all of the main fronts stretching the final limits of Axis strength, even the rear areas of occupied Europe began to erupt. This was especially true in occupied Yugoslavia. After the major defeat of the Slovenian nationalist forces in September, 1943 Leon Rupnik had quickly sought the assistance of the Germans in attempting to reorganize the anti-Communist forces in the country. By the beginning of October, 1943 this new force amounted to 5,000 men and were located in and around Ljubljana. The pro-Mihailovich forces that had been operating in Slovenia (the so-called Blue Guard), now only numbered some 400 men. This number would remain unchanged until the end of the war. By August, 1944 the Home Guard strength had risen to 12,000 men, but by the end

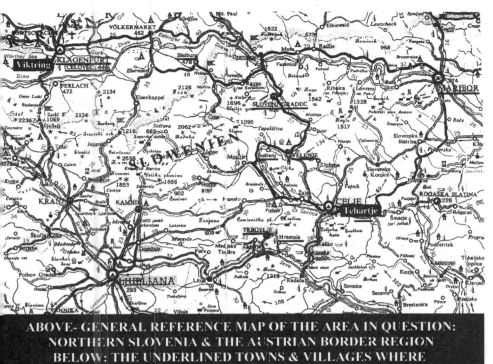

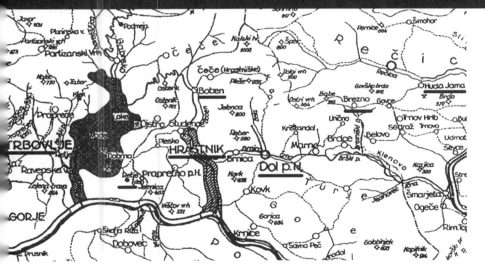

f the war, out of these 12,000 men, ...000 would be dead, most killed ...fter capture. The first instance of a ...assacre of the Home Guard ...ccurred in the Slovenian province ...f Dolenjsko (Unterkrain) when in ...rly May, 1945 the Partisans ...ught a column of retreating ...omobranci and fleeing civilians ...om Primorska, on the coastal ...gion of the country. This column ...as ambushed around Gorisko ...orz) and virtually decimated.

They then grabbed 300 wounded Home Guardsmen from the destroyed column and eventually massacred them in Lesce, by Veldes (Bled). Other, larger killings took place shortly after the war, when the majority of the Home Guard were forced to return to Yugoslavia by the British Army. Bleiburg, located in southern Austria, just across the Yugoslav-Austrian border was the site where the Slovenian 1st, 2nd, 3rd, and 4th Home Guard Regiments

had sought asylum. On May 28th, 1945 the 4th Regiment, together with a Home Guard replacement company, were forcibly sent to Rosenbach, where a contingent of Slovenian partisans assumed control of them. They were to be marched through the Slovenian countryside, many being killed along the way. A day later, on May 29th, it was the 3rd Regiment's turn to head out for Rosenbach and a dark end. On May 30th, it was the turn of the 2nd Regiment, and on May 31st, 500 men from the 1st Regiment were also sent to meet their fate. In Novo Mesto (Rudolfswerth), 1,000 of these returning Home Guard were killed, but the majority of the Slovenian Domobranci met their end in a death march begun at Teharje (Tuechern) by Celje (east-northeast of Ljubljana), and which ended in Trbovlje (southwest of Celje) One more thing should be said about the Slovenian Home Guard: They weren't Fascists, as much as they were anti-Communists. In fact, in 1944 they had hoped that an Allied landing on the Adriatic coast would allow them to switch sides and with American & British support, they would be able to not only expel the Germans, but the Communists as well. It was an illusion, but for the Slovenian nationalists, it was their last hope. Because the Germans knew that the Domobranci nurtured these western feelings, they never quite trusted them fully, and always made sure that their units were supervised. A perfect example of this fear is a German report dated 14th January, 1945 stating that the Home Guard garrison at Bistrica had to be disarmed by the SS on December 30th, 1944.*

----

* NARS Microfilm Series T-501, Roll 261, Frame 000547.

RARE PHOTOGRAPHS OF THE SLOVENIAN AXIS FORCES

This section includes extremely rare photographs of the Domobranci and ethnic German Wehrmannschaft. As with most of the pictures shown in this book, they have never been published before in the English language. They offer an insight into the uniforms, badges and insignia of these Slovenian Axis forces that was heretofore unavailable.

Below Left: The metallic badge insignia for Slovenian communications troops.

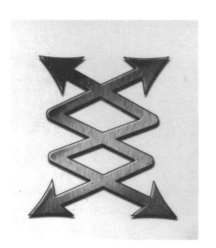

Below Right: The only known photograph showing a Home Guard enlisted man wearing the metallic communications badge. Notice that it was worn on both collar tabs. The uniforms shown are ex-Dutch Army, and the oval soft cover cockade is shown.

Bottom Photo: Ljubljana Stadium, April 20th, 1944. A new batch of Slovenian Policemen are inducted into the nationalist defense forces. Notice that they are all armed with pistols and carry a distinctive head cover.

Above: A graduation phoptograph for a Home Guard platoon. There is one SS officer in the group. A close examination of his cuff band reveals that before being posted to train these Slovenian recruits, he served in the Deutschland SS Regiment. There are also five SS and one German Order police NCO's (noncommissioned officers) in the photograph. Another close examination using a magnifying glass reveals that at least one of them served in the SS Langemarck Regiment. The close association between the supply & support of the Domobranci and the German SS & Police forces can be clearly appreciated by this unique photograph.

Left: Slovenian Domobran sergeants. They were identified as (from left to right) Sergeant Anton Kovacic-Sulc, Sergeant Sustersic, and Sergeant Ivan Zvan. What is interesting is that Sergeant Kovacic-Sulc is wearing German Order Police collar tabs (they all are), but he is also wearing the shoulder boards of a Home Guard sergeant, while his comrades do not have them. Also, Sergeant Zvan (far right) is still wearing the metallic Legion of Death emblem on his soft cover!

Top Right: Home Guard tank crew. The uniform is the ex-Dutch Army, dyed black. The blue, Slovene national eagle (on a white background) is clearly seen.

Below Right: The only known photograph of a variant Home Guard cloth insignia. Instead of using the insignia pictured by the Home Guard tankers above, this cloth insignia featured the national colors, slanted sideways! This is supposedly a photo taken of an SNVZ volunteer, so we can speculate that perhaps this emblem was supposed to help differentiate the soldiers of the SNVZ from those of the Home Guard, but the fact that no other photograph showing this cloth insignia could mean that the idea never took hold. Of course, this is all speculation, and this picture, innocent as it initially seems, is one of the most perplexing photos seen.

Center: The blue and white Slovenian national shield as was worn by all Home Guard forces, except the SNVZ (who had their own shield).
Right: The Home Guard helmet shield worn on the left side of the helmet.
Below: The SNVZ shield.

Left: A Home Guard soldier wearing the last version of the soft cover cockade. It was oval, with the Slovene national colors of white-blue-red, with the Slovenian national eagle in white, superimposed over the colors.

Below, Center Right: A closer examination of this last version of the oval cockade. It appears to have made its appearance in late 1944. General Leon Rupnik, pictured on page 64, is also wearing this cockade.

Bottom: A rare photograph of a Slovenian artillery unit in 1944.

Right: An extremely rare photograph of an SD detachment in Oberkrain (northwestern Slovenia). The men are Slovenians, but notice that all of their insignia, from their shoulder boards to their collar tabs and cap insignia are all SS/SD. The SD recruited other ethnic groups as well. For example, in Croatia they raised 15 such SD companies, distributing them throughout the larger cities and towns.

Wehrmannschaftsregiment Untersteiermark
(Defense Militia Regiment Lower Styria)

When Slovenia was occupied by the Germans and Italians in 1941, the northern half of the country was annexed by Nazi Germany. The ethnic German population in that region (known as Untersteiermark) were formed initially into a paramilitary organization called the Heimatbund. From this group was formed the Wehrmannschaft (Defense Militia). The photo below was taken in Maribor (Marburg), and was dated 17 April, 1942 - when membership in the Militia became mandatory for all ethnic Germans.

Left, Center, & Bottom: Maribor, same date (17 April, 1942). A parade was held by the Wehrmannschaft in order to inaugurate compulsory service. A total number of 87,400 men in Lower Styria were liable for service. What had been a single battalion in 1941, was expanded to several in 1942. Eventually, a regiment of five battalions, made up of the most physically fit soldiers was raised. It fought the partisans from 1942 onwards with varying success.

Left: Same date and occasion. Notice the brassard on these ethnic German men. Some kind of writing appears to be surrounding the the Styrian lion emblem, with what looks like a cross or crown above the lion.

Top Right: April 17th, 1942. Present at the ceremony was SS Oberfuehrer Franz Steindl (center of photo), back from fighting at the front. Notice that he is wearing the "Narvik" shield award on his left upper sleeve. The special cloth Edelweiss, worn on the left side of the mountain cap, is also seen here being worn. This emblem was worn by the Wehrmannschaft on a raspberry red background (see the drawing at center, far right).

Below Left: Many ethnic German families became the object of partisan retribution when they were called to serve in the Defense Militia. Here the Strehar family is escorted from their local village (located just southeast of Ljubljana) by the local SD command for their own safety.

Below Right: The unique belt buckle of the Wehrmannschaft. The helmet is from the Tyrolean militia forces, but reports indicate that the

Oberkrain (Upper Carnolian) ethnic German militia units and the militia units from Untersteiermark also began using these helmets when they were all inducted into the Volkssturm (People's Army) in 1944. The shield, depicting the Styrian lion & sword, with the Nazi swastika beneath a shield, was stencil painted onto the left side of the helmet.

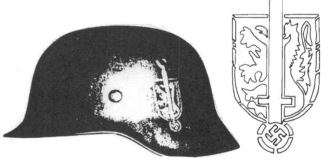

Left: The Wehrmannschaft (Defense Militia) battalions were given courses in military training. One such training was target practice, and the men were supplied with a variety of diverse weapons. Here, a Militiaman practices with the C 96 M712/1932 Mauser, with the detachable stock.

Below: A militiaman practices firing the Yugoslav M37 7.92mm light machine gun. The Wehrmannschaft were supplied with this very abundant ex-Yugoslav Army weapon.

Below: The late-war version of the Wehrmannschaft arm band.

Right: Map courses were also given, especially for the officers and NCO's of the militia companies and battalions.

Right Center: The staff of Defense Militia Battalion "South" outside their headquarters during the spring of 1942. A cross country march was scheduled as part of their training.

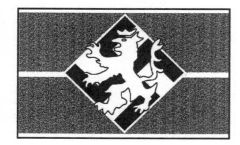

Right: Firing the Yugoslav M37 light machine gun. This view gives us an excellent view of the collar tabs and shoulder boards, which were also red with a white outer trim. The eagle & swastika emblem worn on the mountain caps was metallic, possibly aluminum.

Left: Rifle practice was also a requirement in the Defense Militia. The militia battalions took the place of German occupation forces that would have otherwise been needed to guard against guerrilla attack. At its height, the Wehrmannschaftsregiment Untersteiermark contained around 6,000 men split up into five combat battalions and some minor training companies and posts.

In 1944, when the Regiment was absorbed into the Volkssturm, its five battalions, named "Sued", "Nord", "Ost", "West", and "Mitte", were redesignated in sequential order by Roman numerals: I, II, III, IV, & V.

Left: Schematic Order of Battle for the Regiment. By March, 1945 it could still count on 4,500 able-bodied men within her table of organization.

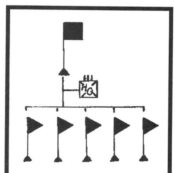

Left Center: The Wehrmannschaft is seen marching through the northern Slovenian countryside, sometime in 1942.

Left: The elder militia soldiers in the group gather for a smoke break. All able bodied ethnic German males between the ages of 17-45 were required to serve with the Defense Militia Regiment Lower Styria. Later, this age limit was expanded include youngsters as young as 15 and 16, and men as old as 60, but this did not occur until late 1944 when the entire male population was called up for the Volkssturm. In 1942, the Oberkrain (Upper Carnolia) region had a total of 17,592 men eligible for service in the Defense Militia.

Right: NSKK, or Nazional-sozialistisches Kraftfahr-korps (National Socialist Motor Transport Corps) - this was the Nazi Party's motorized troops. They served in numerous auxiliary duties. In this case, they happen to be ethnic Germans from Slovenia. They were attached to the "Motorgruppe Alpenland" headquarters, which controlled the following NSKK battalions: In Kaerten- 90th 190th; In Salzburg- 91st & 191st; Steiermark- 88th, 89th, 188th; Tirol Voralberg- 92nd & 192nd.

Center Right: 1943- An ethnic German NSKK column using an outdated Italian CV-33 tankette and German 37mm AT gun.

Bottom Right: The 37mm AT gun being used.

Top Left: The NSKK in Oberkrain (Upper Carinthia) and Untersteiermark (Lower Styria) also employed captured French Army tanks to help police the countryside. Here a platoon of French-made R35 tanks moves down a Slovenian country road. This tank had a top speed of 20 kilometers per hour (11.8 miles per hour), weighed 10.8 tons, and had a 37mm SA 18 AT gun, with an auxiliary 7.5mm machine gun (1931 model). Fully loaded, the R35 tank could carry up to 100 rounds of 37mm AT rounds, and 2,400 rounds of machine-gun ammunition.

Center Left: A closer view of an NSKK crew member. This man was responsible for driving this R35 tank. All of these NSKK photographs were taken in the Slovenian region of Selska dolina between July 25th-27th, 1942.

Bottom Photo: Krainj (Krainburg), September 27th, 1942. The Wehrmannschaft parades through the city. On this day, Dr. Alois Friedrich Rainer announced that the Gorenjska (Oberkrain) region had finally been made quiet. This was a premature announcement!

Top Right: On the night of January 7th-8th, 1943 the German Order Police, Gendarmerie, Wehrmacht, and Wehrmannschaftsbataillon surrounded the Partisan "Pohorje" Battalion at Trije zebli na Pohorju, after the guerrilla unit had been betrayed by local farmers. During the intense battle in which the German forces surrounded and then surprised the Slovenian partisan unit (most of the combatants were asleep when the fight broke out), 66 guerrillas were killed and one was captured, only to be executed later in the month. Here we see members of the Wehrmannschaft marching from the battle scene. This photo was taken on the morning of January 8th, 1943 (after the battle).

Center Right & Below: German Order Police & Wehrmannschaft men examine the dead bodies of the Slovenian guerrillas. The partisans had built permanent wooden bunkers, sunk halfway into the ground, since this heavily forested region (located some 20 kilometers southwest of Maribor, was to be their winter quarters.

INSIGNIA & PLATE ILLUSTRATIONS OF THE SLOVENIAN AXIS FORCES, 1941-1945

The Village Guard (*Vaske Straze*)

The insignia of the village guard was quite simple. It included civilian attire, and perhaps a bandoleer to go along with his Italian rifle. He was issued a small metallic emblem in 1942 which was to be worn on a beret. It was a simple sword and shield and there were exactly three variants as shown below:

The Legion of Death (*Legija Smrti*)

In May, 1942 Major Josip Novak's Slovenian *Chetnik* formation was offically inducted into the Italian MVAC, or *Milizia Voluntare Anti-Communista* (Volunteer Anti-Communist Militia). The formation was christened the *"Legija Smrti"* ("Legion of Death"). Out of 1,687 men in the unit as of February, 1943 only 640 men were Orthodox, while the remainder were Slovenian Catholics who wished to a return of the Serbian King Peter, II. These Catholic volunteers had been added to Major Novak's formation and in this way, 11 companies were formed and eventually grouped into three battalions. The use of berets became more widespread in 1942.

The insignia of the "Legion of Death" was an Italian metallic badge depicting the skull and crossed bones. Another variant, also used was the death's head, with a knife being held by its teeth. Both of these metal insignias was to be worn on the front of the beret or cover.

MVAC insignia was worn on the left side of the beret and included the triangular cloth emblem in various colors, with or without a colored star (depending on rank). Below: The skull insignia of the Legion of Death

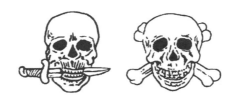

The intermingling of these various metallic insignia between the Village Guard and the Legion of Death happened all too often, and in many cases, it wasn't surprising to see both emblems being worn by the same volunteer! There were also photographic evidence depicting these emblems being worn on the left breast pocket and on the right sleeve. Below right is an example of how a volunteer would wear his insignia:

The uniform of the Legion of Death was as varied as could be. Initially, French, Italian, and Czech helmets were used, as well as the Yugoslav soft cover. Arms included just about the same number of diverse

sources. The use of Yugoslav clothing, mixed in with civilian clothing, and Italian military attire was also a common practice.

In the spring of 1942 the Italians delivered 2,500 used Italian tropical uniforms. These were of a tan or light brown color and had originally been fabricated for use in Italian North Africa. Thousands of black berets were also distributed. One Slovenian source mentions that White Guard officers often were given the better quality Italian officer's uniform, made by the *"Union militare"* firm.

When Italy surrendered on September 8th, 1943 the MVAC formations were left leaderless. Some broke up and went home while others sought further service with the Germans. The Germans began to raise Slovenian units and would eventually clothe them with their own captured or regular stocks, but one unique aspect was that in the beginning of this transitory phase, many Slovenian volunteers serving under the Germans would still wear their old MVAC insignia.

BELOW: A Slovenian Village Guardsman and a member of the Legion of Death, circa 1943

Slovenian Village Guard and Legion of Death 1943

THE SLOVENIAN HOME GUARD (Domobranci)

When the Germans assumed control for the remnants of the Slovenian collaborationist forces, they set out to fully retrain, re-equip, and rearm these units of volunteers.

Initially, the Home Guard (as the White Guard were now called) continued to wear ex-Yugoslav uniforms or the Italian tropical uniforms supplied to them. In the fall of 1943 the first German manufactured cockade, to be worn on the front of the soft cover, was distributed.

This was a very simple, triangular metallic emblem which featured the Slovenian national colors (white-blue-red) in horizontal bars coming across the cap badge. It looked as follows:

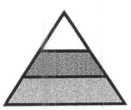

In early 1944 a new, oval cockade was introduced. It was identical to the triangular cockade, except that it was a little larger and was oval in shape:

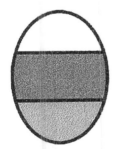

A later version of the oval cockade, introduced in late 1944, included the Slovenian national eagle superimposed over the national colors please see page 69 for a view of this

last version of the forage cap cockade).

The Germans supplied their Slovenian partners with a light grey-green uniform that was acquired from captured Dutch Army stocks. Boots included ankle and riding books, while the helmet was usually the Italian M1933 version. The soft cover (forage cap) was of Dutch origin. The Italian M1933 helmet was given a stenciled decal that was worn on the left side:

Right: The white-blue-red shield that was stenciled on the left side of the Italian (and later on) German helmet.

The cloth insignia which the Home Guard wore on the left sleeve of the tunic was a shield with the Slovenian national eagle in blue on a white background.

THE SLOVENE NATIONAL SECURITY FORCE (Slovenski Narodni Varnostni Zbor)

The uniforms of the SNVZ were primarily Italian in origin, and Italian camouflage uniforms were very much "in style" and sought after, but since the Italian jackets were originally open-styled to allow wearing of shirts and neckties, they began to fasten them below the neck, the German way.

But the memory of the Italian presence was still very much in mind, so much so that many companies took to wearing large, colorful ties the Italian way (like a scarf). Each company would choose one tie color. This was done to differentiate one company from another.

For a shield insignia, they also wore a cloth shield on their left sleeve, but it was not the Slovenian national eagle, but a red Illyrian ship, on a blue sea, and a white background:

The cap cockade and the shoulder boards worn were the same as for the regular Home Guard units. There is enough photographic evidence to show that many SNVZ officers (transferred from the Domobranci to

81

help raise the SNVZ) wore the regular, Dutch army style uniform and soft cover.

THE UPPER CARNOLIA HOME DEFENSE FORCE (Gorenjsko Domobranstvo)

The Upper Carnolia Home Defense Force was a substantially large Slovenian collaborationist organization that was raised, trained, supplied, and supported by the *Gestapo*, or *Geheimstaatspolizei* (State Secret Police).

Only one photograph has so far surfaced, showing a group of these Slovenian volunteers from the *Gorenjska (Oberkrain)* region, and it shows them dressed completely in *Sicherheitspolizei* (SS Security Police) uniform, complete with collar tabs and shoulder boards.

ABOVE: Slovenian volunteers from the Upper Carnolia Region, circa 1944.

DEFENSE MILITIA REGIMENT "LOWER STYRIA" (Wehrmannschaftsregiment "Untersteiermark")

"edelweiss" worn on the side of the cover, were all raspberry red in color:

Left: The Wehrmannschaft belt buckle.

The men used SA ranks and wore an armband that included the Styrian lion in black, surrounded by a white circle, superimposed over a white and green band. This was worn on the left sleeve:

Later, a more stylized arm band was issued and used by the men of the *Wehrmannschaft:*

German mountain boots complete the uniform. Later, when th *Wehrmannschaft* was inducted int the German *Volkssturm* in Octobe 1944 they were given helmets wit the Styrian lion, sword, & swastik stenciled on the left side of th helmet.

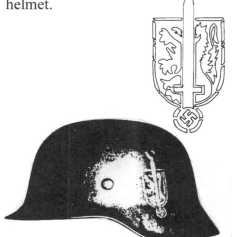

The ethnic German defense militia forces, raised from Slovenians of German/Austrian descent in Gorensjka and Stajerska certainly had quite an interesting uniform. The tunic and trousers were basically styled exactly like the German mountain troop blouse and tunic, and was light brown in color. The cap worn was the German mountain cap. The collar tabs, shoulder boards and the lozenge background of the metallic

THE COLOR PLATES
(front cover, left to right)

Ethnic-German Wehrmannschaft trooper, circa 1942.

He wears a light brown mountain troop uniform, complete with climbing books and mountain cap. He wears an armband on his left sleeve. It depicts the Styrian lion in black on a round, white background-surmounted on a white and green striped background.

His collar tabs, shoulder boards, and the lozenge background to the white metal edelweiss insignia (worn on the left side of the mountain cap) are all made of the same raspberry red cloth.

The national eagle, worn on the front of the mountain cap, is a white metallic. His belt buckle and holster are all black leather. He is aiming his C96 M712/1932 Mauser with the attached gun stock .

Legion of Death Volunteer : September, 1942

This volunteer is wearing a variety of clothing which includes ex-Yugoslav Army trousers, leggings, and footwear, French helmet, and civilian shirt. He carries a canteen and small pouch, including a blanket rolled over his shoulder. His weapon appears to be holding the Yugoslav "karabinka" M 24 7.92mm rifle.

SNVZ Volunteer (kneeling), circa 1944

This Slovene National Security Force trooper is wearing an Italian camouflage patter jacket and trouser. His companions wore mainly Italian attire, but favored both German and Italian camouflage patterns (including German camouflage covers). The SNVZ cloth insignia (a red Illyrian ship, on a blue sea and white background) is seen being worn on the left sleeve of the jacket. He is wearing the grey-green soft cover of ex-Dutch army origin, with the metallic oval national cockade being worn on the front of the cover. The cockade bears the Slovene national colors of (from top to bottom) white-blue-red. His weapon is the Italian 9mm Beretta (1938 A model). This submachine gun could fire at the rate of 600 rounds per minute. The shoulder boards were standard Home Guard insignia.

Slovenian Home Guard Volunteer, circa 1944

The *Domobranci* wore a grey-green uniform, supplied by the Germans from captured ex-Dutch Army stocks. His helmet was the Italian M1933 version, complete with the Slovene national colors stenciled onto a shield, worn on the left side of the helmet. The Slovenian national eagle was worn on the left sleeve. It was embroidered using blue thread for the eagle on a white background. footwear and leggings were of Italian origin, although towards the end of 1944 German footwear also came into use. Again, his weapon is the Italian M 1938 Beretta. His uniform is completed by the use of Slovene Home Guard shoulder boards.

(back cover, left to right)

Legion of Death Commander, early 1943

This officer wears a combination of civilian and Italian army gear. The jacket is a very stylish civilian cut which he has chosen to wear with his newly supplied Italian tropical trousers of a tan or light brown color. Two thousand five-hundred of these uniforms were supplied to the White Guard beginning in 1942. His arm patch is also a modified version, and seems to have been a one-of-a-kind item, and simple arm bands with a black and white skull and crossed bones emblem were more common. He wears a black beret, also supplied by the Italians, and although he is authorized to wear the skull and crossed bones metallic emblem on the front of the beret, he is also wearing the "Village Guard" metal emblem ("sword and shied") as well. On the side of the beret is the emblem used by the Italian MVAC (*Milizia Voluntare Anti-Comunista*), or Volunteer Anti-Communist Militia units. He is a squad commander because he is wearing a red star on a white triangular cloth [see page 16 of this book for the complete MVAC rank description]. His pistol and belt buckle are all of Italian origin. Italian black riding boots rounded up his uniform.

Ethnic-German Wehrmannschaft trooper, circa 1944

This soldier wears the same basic uniform, with the exception that he is wearing the late-version arm band on his left sleeve. It featured the Styrian lion in white, superimposed over a tilted, black swastika. The lion and swastika are enclosed in a hooked, white background, surrounded by to horizontal green fields separated by thin, white fields. His weapon is the famous German 7.92mm 98 K (carbine). At this time the Whermannschaft were issued with German steel helmets, with a stylized Styrian lion, sword, and swastika, on a shield, stenciled using white paint on the left side of the helmet.

Village Guard Officer, late 1942

By 1942 the Slovenian Village Guard had been given a semblance of a uniform. Here this officer is wearing the Italian tropical uniform, complete with black beret, brown leather belt and pistol holster, and black Italian riding boots. He wears the metallic "sword & shield" emblem of the Village Guard on his black beret. The tie and shirt were usually black and white (respectively) and were civilian in origin. The winter uniform, used also for special occasions by the White Guard forces was a long, black greatcoat for the enlisted ranks and black riding trousers and blouse for the officers. The shirt was white and the tie was black.

THE SHIELDS (left to right)

Home Guard helmet decal, worn on the left side of the helmet.
Home Guard national eagle emblem, worn of the left sleeve.
SNVZ cloth insignia, worn on the left sleeve.

———————————

BELOW: a larger view of the map that is featured on page 65 of this book. The Slovenian nationalist forces, along with the retreating Croatian Army and Serbian Chetnik units, withdrew into Austria during late April, early May, 1945. The majority ended at Bleiburg and Klagenfurt, but other, smaller numbers of troops crossed at other points on the Austro-Slovene border.

The Northern Slovene Border Region (including the Austrian border)

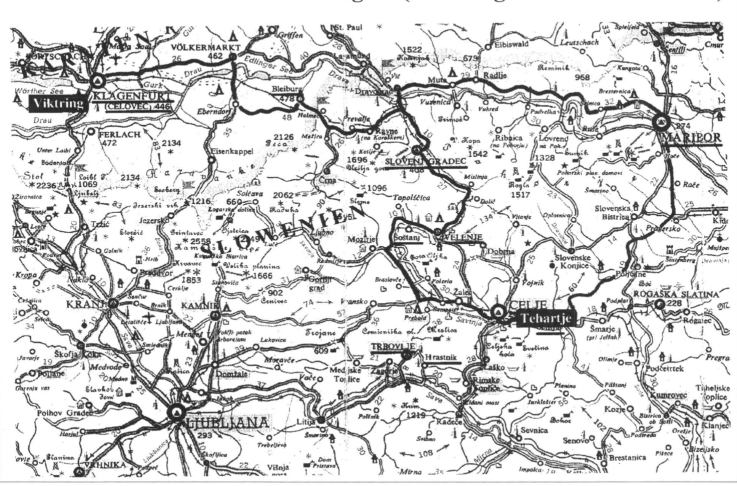

Axis Europa Magazine:

THE ONLY ENGLISH LANGUAGE JOURNAL TOTALLY DEVOTED TO WWII AXIS MILITARY HISTORY!

If Axis Military history interests you, then you should try a sample copy of our color journal:

Domestic Sample Copy:	8.00 Dollars
Canadian Sample Copy	9.00 Dollars
All Other Foreign:	10.00 Dollars

Yearly subscriptions to the journal:

Domestic Subscribers:	$20.00 Dollars
CanadianSubscribers:	$24.00 Dollars
Foreign Subscribers:	$30.00 Dollars

AXIS EUROPA BOOKS:

Axis Europa magazine also has a growing line of World War II Axis military history books. Here are but three samples of books currently being prepared:

"Slovenian Axis Forces in WWII, 1941-1945" text by Antonio Munoz, color & b/w line drawings by renowned military artist, Vincent Wai.

"Baltic Lions: The Estonian Army in World War II" by Jukka Mattila, color & b/w line drawings by Finnish artist Marko Tiainin.

"Flottiglia Nostra: The Decima MAS & the Italian Social Republic, 1943-1945" by Prof. Marco Novarese.

is Europa magazine is published using glossy, full color heavy 'd stock covers and 70lb. glossy coated paper for the inside ges. Each issue comes chuck full of fresh and new articles on military history of the Axis Forces.

is Europa is *not* a revisionist organ. We scrutinize every mission to make sure that what you will read is pure military ts- no fiction, and no politics!

r editorial staff is composed of some of the best writers in the ld of Axis military history. Many are published authors like x Trye *("Mussolini's Soldiers")*, Philip S. Jowett *("Chinese rlord Armies")*, Antonio Munoz *("Forgotten Legions")*, dris Kursietis *("Hungarian Army in WWII")*, Adam Geibel, . In addition to our feature articles, we publish regular columns each issue: Axis Air Forces, Axis Medals & Badges, Axis litary Hardware, Empire of Japan, Book Review section, etc.

ur yearly subscription gives you access to the very best in Axis itary articles, and book reviews geared for this specific subject tter. You also get the latest news regarding new and upcoming is Europa books. Although Axis Europa concentrates on the is allies, we also publish articles on about the German Armed ces.

ypical comment about our latest issue:
ntastic! the journal just keeps getting better & better!"

Please make all payments out to "Axis Europa"
WE ACCEPT Domestic CHECKS, **or** VISA / MC

name:
address:
city/state:
country/zip code:
credit card number
expiration date:
signature:
Do you wish a catalogue of books? YES / NO
I'd like a one year subscription:
I'd like a sample copy:
NY State Residents, Please add sales tax:
Grand Total:

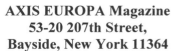

AXIS EUROPA Magazine
53-20 207th Street,
Bayside, New York 11364

About Axis Europa

Axis Europa was established in January, 1995 by military historian and author, Antonio J. Munoz. The company was formed because of what seemed to be ageneral lack of readily available data on the "minor" Axis forces which fought on the side of Germany during the Second World War. The term "minor" Axis is deceptive, since our research has brought to light facts which make it perfectly clear that without these so-called "minor" forces, Germany could not have sustained her war effort for as long as she did.

The company publishes books dealing strictly with the subject of World War II Axis Military History. We do not cover the political or social aspects since there are sufficient books and magazines that cover these two aspects. We are not revisionists! We are only concerned with covering the military history of the Axis forces from an objective and un-biased point of view. We also publish a color journal dealing with the same subject matter. Our author's come from various countries: the US, Canada, Britain, The Netherlands, Finland, Italy, Croatia, etc.

The company has recently published its first ever purely German-oriented book ("The German Police"). In the future, we plan on producing more such books. Axis Europa fills a gap which no other firm has attempted to cover before: The field of NEW data on the military history of the Axis forces. One of our specialties is the sub-topic of foreign volunteers of the Wehrmacht and Waffen-SS. This is a fascinating area of study dealing with a huge foreign volunteer movement. We offer many titles on this particular subject.

We hope that once you see our list of books and magazines, you will agree with us that our line is unique and an important contribution to the military history of the Second World War.

Antonio J. Munoz
Publisher.

Shipping information:

NOTE: FOR OVERSEAS AIR MAIL - Each book weighs approximately ½ pound each, except book numbers "1" and "11" which weigh 4 pounds each.

Domestic: Book Rate: $5.00 1st book, $2.00 each additional; USPS Priority: $6.00 1st book, $3.00 each additional book. UPS Ground: 10.00 1st book, $3.00 each additional book.

Canadian: Surface charges are $4.00 for the 1st book, $3.00 each additional book. Air Mail (use Overseas Air mail rates, below).

Overseas: Surface - $10.00 for the 1st book, $3.00 each additional. BOOK DEALERS & STORES: Please check M-Bag rates (Call for quotes).

AIR MAIL OVERSEAS: 1 lb.= $7.20/ 2 lbs.= $12.00/ 3 lbs.= $16.80/ 4 lbs.= $21.60 5 lbs.= $26.40/ 6 lbs.= $31.20/ 7 lbs.= $36.00/ 8 lbs.= $40.80 9 lbs.= $45.60/ 10 lbs.= $50.40/ 11 lbs.= $55.20/ 12 lbs.= $64.48

Example: If you ordered one copy of Book No.11 and one copy each of book Nos. 2, 5, 9, & 10, the total (approximate) weight of your package would be 6 lbs. (pounds). The cost to ship AIR MAIL overseas would therefore be $31.20 .**NOTE: Air Mail shipping to Pacific Rim & Middle Eastern countries is 10% higher,** so this 6 lb. package would cost $34.32 to send to a country like New Zealand, or Saudi Arabia (as examples).

Terms of Sale: All sales are final. We accept a returned item only at our discretion and only after you have contacted us in writing. Please do not return any books or magazines without first writing to us and stating the problem. We will decide if the situation merits a refund and then we will only give CREDIT or PARTIAL CREDIT towards any other Axis Europa product. Re-stocking, re-packaging and end user fees may apply.

NEW YORK STATE RESIDENTS: You MUST include local sales tax. Axis Europa must (like all NYS businesses) file form T-100 with the New York State Tax office every three months.

INSURANCE: Insurance is not available to foreign orders. We suggest that you order using

AIR MAIL which is the safest form of shipping.Domestic insurance rates:
If your order is under $100.00, then your insurance cost is $2.00
If your order is under $200.00, then your insurance cost is $3.00
If your order is under $300.00, then your insurance cost is $4.00
You must state if you wish insurance in your order and payment for insurance must be included.
NOTE: WE ARE NOT RESPONSIBLE FOR UN-INSURED PARCELS.

HOW TO PLACE AN ORDER:
We accept VISA or Mastercard credit card orders. We also accept <u>domestic</u> checks, but Canadian, Mexican, and other foreign & overseas checks <u>must</u> <u>be</u> <u>depositable</u> <u>in</u> <u>s</u> <u>US</u> <u>bank.</u> International Postal Giros (Money Orders), or Bank Drafts are also acceptable. Cash can be sent, but it is sent at the customer's own risk. While we accept cash, we do not recommend this form of payment.

CREDIT CARD ORDERS:
When placing a credit card order you must supply the following information: (1) Full name as it appears on the card (please print), (2) complete address, (3) card number, (4) expiration date of card, (5) items wanted, (6) type of shipping wanted (air or surface), and (7) signature*

* Credit card orders sent via e-mail, or by phone order cannot, by virtue of their modality, include your signature, but will be accepted.

METHOD OF ORDER: If ordering by check, cash, bank draft, or postal money order, you can mail your order in to us. If ordering by Visa or Mastercard, you can mail, phone in, fax, e-mail, or go to our web page (http://members.aol.com /axiseuropa) and use the on-line order form. We do not accept "walk-in" purchases without a prior appointment.

AXIS EUROPA MAGAZINE BACK ISSUES:
The following is a list of the major articles found in our journal. All back issues are low in quantity. Once an issue is sold out. It will only be available in Photocopy format, so please hurry and place your back issue orders now!

ISSUE 1 - Serbian State & Frontier Guard (pt.1), Croatian Army in WWII (pt.1).
ISSUE 2 - Serbian State & Frontier Guard (pt.2), Croatian Army in WWII (pt.2), The Sword of Islam: The History of the 13.Waffen-Gebirgs-Division der-SS "Handschar" (pt.1).
ISSUE 3 - Croatian Army in WWII (pt.3), The Sword of Islam (pt.2), On the Cuff: The British Legion of St. George, Teutonic Magyars: Hungarian Volunteers of the Waffen-SS (pt.1).
ISSUE 4 - Croatian Army in WWII (pt.4), The Croatian Legion in Russia, Teutonic Magyars (pt.2), The Italian Decima X MAS in Russia, History of the Bosnian SS "Kama" Division, Croatian Troops Then & Now, Estonian Troops Then & Now.
ISSUE 5 - Croatian Army in WWII (pt.5), Teutonic Magyars (pt.3), For King & Fatherland: The History of the Montenegro Volunteer Corps (pt.1), German Police & Auxiliary Forces in Poland, 1939-1945 (pt.1), Serbian Troops Then & Now.
ISSUE 6 - Croatian Army in WWII (pt.6), Teutonic Magyars (pt.4), For King & Fatherland (pt.2), German Police & Auxiliary Forces in Poland, 1939-1945 (pt.2), Italian Elite: The Xth Decima MAS Division, 1943-1945 (pt.1).
ISSUE 7 - Croatian Army in WWII (pt.7), Teutonic Magyars (pt.5), For King & Fatherland (pt.3), German Police & Auxiliary Forces in Poland, 1939-1945 (pt.3), Italian Elite (pt.2), WWII Axis Military Postage Stamps, Slovenian Troops Then & Now.
ISSUE 8 - Croatian Army in WWII (pt.8), Teutonic Magyars (pt.6), For King & Fatherland (pt.4), Latvian Volunteers of the Waffen-SS & Order Police, 1941-1945.
ISSUE 9 - Croatian Army in WWII (pt.9), The Moslem Legion of the Sandjak, Albanian Collaborationist Forces 1943-44, New pictures of the Kaminski Brigade.
ISSUE 10 - Legion Stamp Propaganda: Axis Military Postage Stamps & Postcards, 1941-45, Uniforms & Insignia of the Croatian Air Force

Legion, 1941-1945, Romania: A Brave Ally 1941-1944, Albanian Fascist Militia (revisited).

ISSUE 11 - The Carpathian (Ukranian) Sic Units - 1939, The Arab Fascist Youth of Lybia, The Italian Expeditionary Corps in Russia 1941-42, German Police & Auxiliary Forces in Poland 1939-1945 (pt.4).

ISSUE 12 - The Situation in the Air: Italian East Africa 1940-1941, Latvian Schutzmannschaft Battalions 1941-1945, Artillery Barrage at Taipaleenjoki (Finland), The Battle of Sikniemi (Finland), Volkssturm & Alarm Units in the Eastern Military Districts - January 1945.

ISSUE 13 - Bir El Gobi: The Italian 132nd Tank Regiment's After Action Report, 19 November 1941, The Italian 132nd Armored Division ARIETE, Axis Armor Column: The Italian M13/40 & 14/41 tanks, Axis Medals Column: The Italian Memorial Badge for Service on the Russian Front, The Call in the Wilderness: The Axis Surrender in Tunisia 12-13 May 1943, Paracadutisti: Italian Parachute Units of WWII, Oriental Axis Column: Japan's Allies in Asia, Police & Internal Security Forces of Fascist Italy, 1922-1945, Axis Air Column: Eagles of the Tatras, the Slovak Air Force 1939-45, Another Pilot Down: The Death of Istvan Horthy, Deputy Regent of Hungary, 33.Waffen-Grenadier-Division dèr-SS CHARLEMAGNE.

ISSUE 14- Japan's Mongol Horsemen, French-SS in Berlin, The Slovak Uprising, American Volunteers in Italy's Blackshirt Legion, The Italian Army in Russia, Italian African Police Courses for the SS, Italian Submarine Crew Badge, Against Stalin & Stalinism: Count Grigori vo Lambsdorf, Lithuania's Nazi Police Battalions, The Hungarian Toldi Tanks, Italy's Submarine War, The Battle for Leros, 1943, Indian Volunteers in the German & Italian Army, the Romanian I80 fighter in WWII, book reviews.

Back Issue Costs:
Domestic price: $8.50
Canadian price: $9.50
Overseas price: 10.50

SAVE MONEY! SPECIAL SALE
ORDER ALL BACK ISSUES:
FROM ISSUES 1-14 FOR THE FOLLOWING PRICE:
Domestic: $110.00

Canadian: $120.00
Overseas: $130.00
NOTE: SHIPPING IS ALREADY INCLUDED IN ALL BACK ISSUE ORDERS!

-BOOKS-
1] Forgotten Legions: Obscure Combat Formations of the Waffen-SS, 1943-1945.
ISBN 0-87364-646-0
$58.00 hardcover, dj, 424pp
2] The Kaminski Brigade: A History, 1941-1945.
ISBN 1-891227-02-5 $20.00 sc, 64pp
3] Lions of the Desert: Arab Volunteers in the German Army, 1941-1945.
ISBN 1-891227-03-3 $18.00 sc, 36pp
4] Slovenian Axis Forces in World War II, 1941-1945.
ISBN 1-891227-04-1 $22.00 sc, 88pp
5] For Croatia & Christ: The Croatian Army in World War II, 1941-1945.
ISBN 1-891227-05-X $20.00 sc, 80pp
6] Herakles & The Swstika: Greek Volunteers in the German Army, Police & SS, 1943-1945.
ISBN 1-891227-06-8 $19.00 sc, 68pp
7] Forgotten Legions Booklet.
ISBN 1-891227-07-6   spiralbound, $17.00
NOTE: Only recommended if you have "Forgotten Legions", the hardcover book.
8] The Hungarian Army & its Military Leadership in World War II.
ISBN 1-891227-08-4 $18.00 sc, 62pp
9] Hitler's Eastern Legions, Vol.I - The Baltic Schutzmannschaft.
ISBN 1-891227-09-2 $21.00 sc, 76pp
10] Hitler's Eastern Legions, Vol.II - The Osttruppen.
ISBN 1-891227-10-6 $24.00 sc, 52pp
11] The German Police
ISBN 1-891227-11-4 $42.00 sc, 442pp
12] Eastern Troops in Zeeland, The Netherlands, 1943-1945.
ISBN 1-891227-00-9
13] Russian Volunteers in Hitler's Army, 1941-1945.
1-891227-01-7 $13.00 sc, 60pp
14] Hrvatski Orlovi: Paratroopers of the Independent State of Croatia, 1942-1945.
ISBN 1-891227-13-0 $18.00 sc, 70pp

WRITE US FOR A FULL CATALOG